Sociocybernetics and Political Theory in a Complex World

Sociocybernetics and Complexity

Volumes published in this Brill Research Perspective are listed at *brill.com/rpsc*

Sociocybernetics and Political Theory in a Complex World

Recasting Constitutionalism

By

Roberto Mancilla

BRILL

LEIDEN | BOSTON

This paperback book edition is simultaneously published as issue 1.1 (2020) of *Sociocybernetics and Complexity*, DOI:10.1163/25900587-12340001.

Library of Congress Control Number: 2020941715

Typeface for the Latin, Greek, and Cyrillic scripts: "Brill". See and download: brill.com/brill-typeface.

ISBN 978-90-04-44098-2 (paperback)
ISBN 978-90-04-44127-9 (e-book)

This book is printed on acid-free paper and produced in a sustainable manner.

Contents

Sociocybernetics and Political Theory in a Complex World

Recasting Constitutionalism

Roberto Mancilla
National Autonomous University of Mexico (UNAM), Mexico City, Mexico
robi357@hotmail.com

Abstract

Many of the basic concepts of political science and law were conceived during the Middle Ages, but were not adapted to the current times. The purpose of this study is to address this incongruity by incorporating ideas of cybernetics and complexity theory with political and constitutional theory in order to reconstitute it. In this process, the author offers a basic model of human sociability and alternative frameworks to the idea of the state, the constitution and the way it is applied in the separation of powers, the public/private distinction and constitutionalism.

Keywords

cybernetics – sociocybernetics – complexity – constitutional theory – constitutional law – legal theory – political theory

General Introduction

The Aim of This Study

In *Beyond Camelot*, Edward Rubin argues that many of the basic concepts of political science and Law were conceived during the Middle Ages, and states that they do not adapt to the current times and with the reality that surrounds the administrative state (Rubin, 2005, pp. 1–3). I wish to expand on this point to state that not only the institutions that we use but the way in which social organization is thought of is outdated.

 | DOI:10.1163/9789004441279_002

This premise is further challenged in that we are faced with a reality that goes beyond the state: a globalized world, in the midst of a climate crisis and with rapid technological development that is not always followed by efforts to regulate it, or it is done so in an inconsistent manner across different countries.

What all these phenomena have in common is that they are *complex* – a popular word in the sciences as of late – but that will matter greatly in the future, as all of them unfold. However, a prevailing issue with the term is that there is a lack of a definition that can be ascribed to all purposes. Depending on the system studied, its environment and the qualities of the entity making the observation, a system may or may not be considered "complex"; or, put in another way, "Complexity is in the eye of the beholder" (Northrop, 2010, p. xii). Suffice it to say that complexity is relative, graded and system- and observer-dependent, and that whoever studies it requires a flexible framework in order to cope with it.

Rubin attempts to make his reconstruction by means of the usage of engineering concepts and terms, and I think that he falls short in this effort, as he is not using the right tool for the job. Sure, engineering is knowledge that has allowed for the creation of machines and structures of different sorts in order to fulfill goals and cope with varying environments, but it is not something tailored to human beings.

Furthermore, because they stem from the Enlightenment and the underlying epistemology differs from what we have learned from the advances of cognitive science, another problem that many concepts of social and political theory bear is that they do not communicate with knowledge of the biology of animals and human sociability.

The research topic at hand is the reconstruction of concepts of social organization in the context of phenomena that are complex in nature, and taking into account the biological aspects of sociability. This I will attempt to do with the insights that sociocybernetics can provide, for it is ideal to understand complexity, as the observer and the perspective it generates are part of its approach, and it has a strong foundation in epistemology.

This is obviously a broad agenda that cannot be implemented in the space so generously provided, but is something that hopefully can be expanded and worked on by many others and in different ways. The main goals of this research are the following:

- Carry out a systematic reconstruction of social theory in order to make rigid knowledge flexible, and adequate for the times.
- Open scientific thought in general and in what pertains to the social.
- Avoid simplification and reductionism in social and political theory, which mutilate knowledge and lead to false conclusions.
- Provide a brief look at all the things sociocybernetics has to offer.

Structure

In the first part I will make an introduction to cybernetics that also covers all the concepts that are necessary to assimilate this study; this will ease the flow of reading. I will address what cybernetics is, both in what is called first-order and second-order, as well as its historical development. Sociocybernetics and complex systems theory will also be briefly explained.

Cybernetics has a long and storied tradition, as it gave way to modern computers and many aspects of current technology that we presuppose; however, it is much more than that and extends to the study of cognition, life, social behavior and more. If we are to refurbish political theory with a framework akin to current times, we might as well do it with something as robust as cybernetics, instead of analogies with engineering that might be more quickly exhausted.

I will also examine concepts that are necessary to understand the rest of the study. Recursion, causality, and feedback are the bedrock of first-order cybernetics and they presuppose circularity, where cause and effect are linked with one another. Despite the fact that circular reasoning is seen as a fallacy in logic, the programming of computers can be as complex as it is, due to the fact that it uses a reasoning where the solution of the problem is dependent on smaller iterations of the latter. These concepts are vital for understanding the second part.

Variety and self-organization are also important: The first is the measure of how a system can respond to its environment, and how the latter can influence the former. The second is the way in which this interaction takes place, be it a dynamic of stabilization, one of uncertainty and chaos or the achievement of a state of dynamic equilibrium. This part will be useful in understanding how the state can be theorized as a Viable System Model.

Networks are a better-known concept than the ones I have stated in prior paragraphs, and are more than a collection of interconnected computers, as is colloquially considered. They are the representation of the relations between objects or subjects, and permeate almost everything we do: your social circle (family and friends) is a network, the city you live in is another, and your brain itself is a self-organized network of neurons.

This, then, will show us how the separation of powers is better understood as a network of governmental organs, rather than a simplistic trinity between the legislative, executive and judiciary.

The way we understand things and how we group them together in order to build a larger view or framework will be addressed in the section pertaining to concepts and categories. This at times is something we take for granted, and when we make it conscious, helps us to deconstruct the social frameworks that surround us. In the case of our study, this will be a valuable tool to understand the details that underlie the distinction between what is public and private.

Lastly, complexity as a concept is studied in order to understand the scope of what will be proposed as constitutionalism. Despite the fact that there has been a debate in complex systems theory as to what the measure of complexity is, it is important to know that the latter will depend on the context that it is applied to. Different contexts will lead to different views of complexity; this also applies to constitutionalism, for the limitation of power varies with the subject that it is imposed on.

In the second part I will engage in a general model of human sociability that I call the *3 by 3 by 3 model*, where I depart from all cognition general to all living systems, and transition to human cognition, then to general sociability, and finally, to that of human beings. Much of constitutional theory presupposes epistemological approaches that have no empirical correlation, and thus, this part establishes general concepts that will pervade the rest of this study.

These first two parts comprise a basic section that supplies all the elements needed to rebuild constitutional theory, while the latter endeavor takes place from the third to the seventh part. This takes the form of a critical dismantling of the main tenets of constitutionalism: the state, the constitution, the separation of powers, and the public/private distinction, to then offer reconstructions of each and every one.

The third part deconstructs the idea of the state as a stable and fixed arrangement, in order to use variety and the Viable System Model (VSM) to understand it as a flexible arrangement that presupposes an environment it reacts to, achieving through such efforts a state of equilibrium, which is subject to change as time passes, or losing its viability. That is, the state is rebuilt as a dynamic entity.

The constitution is also thought of as an enduring and fixed thing, instead of seeing it as a document that is interpreted over time and which constructs and remakes its scope and meaning; that is, I propose in the fourth part a constitutional order model that makes use of circular causality and a broader understanding of how to apply the Supreme Law.

In the fifth we build up both on the cybernetic concepts explained in the first part and the recasting made in prior parts in order to deconstruct the idea of the separation of powers, and subsequently propose an alternative – a distribution of function model – that is as dynamic and fluid as prior proposals. The model uses network theory, variety, and the Viable System Model.

The sixth part delves into collective cognition in order to examine the limitations of the public/private distinction; a mobile/geographic distinction as a category will be offered to the reader and it has the benefit of being much more flexible and adaptable to the nuances of a globalized world.

The final part ties all of these ideas together to propose a new understanding of constitutionalism, one that can recognize different territorial and mobile social units, adapting to each and every one, that eventually coalesce into a world system. All of this ties together with cybernetics and with the idea of complexity. This proposal will be called complex constitutionalism.

SECTION 1

Introduction

This section of our study is an introduction to sociocybernetics, which is needed for recasting constitutionalism, which I intend to do; it is also vital, as political theory presupposes notions of the social and of human cognition. If we are to rebuild a framework, we are to start with what underlies it.

With that in mind, we begin with the concepts of cybernetics, sociocybernetics and complexity theory, which all share particular characteristics, and have the virtue of traversing all aspects of science. There are no gaps, as it happens – for instance, between the social and biological sciences, which have their own methods and perspectives.

For this purpose, in the second part I will offer a model that I call *3 by 3 by 3*, which is a practical schema for understanding human social organization in a way that complies with aspects of cognition that are general to all living systems. It helps explain the biological foundations of social behavior: human sociability cannot be understood without a study of its cognition, which at the same time cannot be understood without notions of cognition and sociability that are general to all living systems.

For this purpose, it is comprised of three elements, which at the same time have three triads each, which also have three sets of elements. This means that on a first level, there are three elements, on a second we have nine, and on a third we have twenty-seven. This can be stated as follows:

- *Living systems*: Understood as systems capable of self-replication and cognition; consciousness as the coordination of information and processing will be added; living systems in their goal-directedness are adaptive, as they are thermodynamically open and need to derive energy from their surroundings.
    - *Perception*: Refers to the sensing and interpreting that a living system makes of its surroundings, with there being a threshold of a minimum and maximum of stimuli.
        - *Spatial perception*: Refers to the subjective perception that a living being has of two- and three-dimensional objects.

        - *Temporal perception*: Subjective perception of the duration of the continuous unfolding of events.
        - *Memory*: Capacity to remember past experiences in order to make use of them.
    - *Conceptualizing*: Refers to the information creation process that a living system utilizes. As we perceive things, we create concepts about them with our bodies as a point of reference – that is, the reality that we experience becomes information.
        - *Differentiation*: To distinguish one thing from another.
        - *Meaning assignation*: Once a thing is differentiated from another, we explain to ourselves what the object is and its relation to us.
        - *Embodiment*: Refers to the fact that anything that a living system experiences, understands and conceives, it does so in reference to its own body.
    - *Consciousness*: The intertwining of information created by cognition and perception into an experience of the self which is used by living systems to deal with the reality that surrounds it, and to generate further information.
        - *Self-computation*: The integration of the "I" as subjective experience and the "me" as the objectification of the subject into the self; at the same time, identity influences consciousness as it functions as its frame of reference.
        - *Access-consciousness*: The experiential state where information can be employed and retrieved by means of introspection, and can be used for verbal communication, deliberation, and self-control.
        - *Phenomenal-consciousness*: The experiential state where the totality of its experiential properties is "what it is like" to have it. It cannot be defined in a non-circular way.
- *Human cognition*: One that has a deeper degree of self-reference – it incorporates *teleology* because humans can give a purpose to things and to themselves, and *teleonomy* because it requires constant adaptation to an environment in order to survive. This all means that this type of cognition is reflexive, for there is an internal dimension of the self to which a finality can be assigned and which comprises an internal observation.
    - *Experiential cognition*: Refers to the type of cognition made without sequential steps; it is a "felt" type of thinking and is used to derive knowledge and to interact with the environment.
        - *Perception*: Comprises the identification and processing of sensory information.

- *Intuition*: The experience of grasping an object, not only in a physical way, but rather in a felt way; that is, there is a process of experiencing things.
- *Feelings*: Subjective experience of emotion.

◦ *Logical cognition*: A set of sequential steps that is formed by two or more judgments, ordered in a way such that the latter can be inferred from the former.

- *Reasoning*: Done with certain principles and procedures that give rigor to said thought process.
- *Conceptualizing*: Consists of the interplay of differentiation and meaning assignation.
- *Language*: Understood as a self-referential abstraction, in that "Language is a special system of communication that can talk about itself" (von Foerster, 1994, 116); it is used to cognize and as a means of cognitively processing the environment.

◦ *Cognitive coherence*: The mediation of logical and experiential cognition in a way that permits reflexivity; that is, this type of cognition entails the mediation of feelings and reason in order to create a coherent narrative of the self, as devoid of contradictions as possible.

- *Rationality*: The human capacity to make sense of things and retain the coherence of its cognitive domain.
- *Consciousness as subjective coordination of information*: Human beings, like all living beings, unify all information from perception and cognition (von Foerster, 1979, 1), but unlike them, they can become self-conscious by means of language as an instrument of objectification (Morin, 2008, p. 78): there is a fully objectified internal dimension, that is, humans have a body and experience having a body.
- *Consciousness as subjective story generation*: As human beings are subjective, being the center of what they perceive and understand, one of the features of a conscious subjective being is the creation of a coherent narrative where they are the protagonists. This is the basis for the creation of the narrative of a "we".

- *Human social systems*: In general, social systems consist in the relationship between two or more observers, and thus they comprise mutual observation. These systems have an inherent tension between the self and the other – for I can only be myself and not someone else, and vice versa – and their goal-directedness is teleonomical due to adaptive need, and teleological in the creation of collective goals that go beyond, but are mediated by the latter. Human social systems will be understood in a triadic relation between the continued existence of the system (viability), the establishment of overall goals (optimality) and the mediation between both (adequacy).

- *Viability*: The most basic adaptive behavior that ensures the continued existence of a social group, be it big or small.
  - *Normative order*: The creation of basic rules for the coexistence of the group.
  - *Satisfaction of material needs at household level*: The way in which the goods of the group are divided in order to satisfy the basic collective needs at the household level.
  - *Determination of authority and power*: Consists of seeing who can wield what type of authority within a group and for which purpose.
- *Optimality*: Comprises the goals that a group gives to itself beyond mere survival, taking into account that there are always minorities, and that there can be discrimination against other sectors of the group. That is, it is not a rational process and factors like emotions and ego can interfere.
  - *Identity and history*: There is a group identity, sense of origin, and common destiny which bind the collective together.
  - *Distribution of resources on an overall scale past the basic satisfactions*: Consists in the way in which resources are allocated once the basic needs of many, if not most of the members of a social group are met.
  - *Ideology*: The conception of what constitutes an ideal goal or direction for the overall social system.
- *Adequacy*: The mediation between survival and other group goals.
  - *Problem-solving*: Those with authority have to see to the solving of problems common to all, or those broad enough that they affect a sizable group.
  - *Concessions to individuals and groups*: General concessions such as individual and social rights are made to specific groups or to the generality.
  - *Mobilization of interests and negotiation*: Specific groups and factions within the whole of society mobilize in order to demand rights or a different type of treatment.

One of the main features of this model is that it is recursive, for it is defined in terms of itself, or in this case, its own elements: human social systems presuppose living systems and human cognition; human cognition presupposes human sociability and the cognition of living systems; however, the latter do not presuppose the other two. All of the nine elements of the second triadic level are recursive within their own categories: for instance, with living systems, perception, conceptualization, and consciousness all presuppose each other; they also presuppose one another in the same way as the first level.

On the third level, 27 elements presuppose one another within their own subcategory, and also presuppose those elements in the other subcategories. All of these recursive triads, when correlated, create a matrix in which we can apply just about any topic of human sociability. Issues like feelings, mental health, body image, normalization processes, the identity of an individual vis-à-vis a group's and vice versa can all be understood within it.

This gives the reader a minimal and flexible framework that allows them to understand the biological foundations of social systems, and also how different issues within it can correlate with one another in varied ways. And as it includes aspects of linguistics and semiotics, the practitioners of these disciplines can use these frameworks in the context of their own fields to further their understanding of social systems in general.

In turn, this will give us the foundation to recast constitutionalism, as it will lend us a clear transdisciplinary socio-biological framework for human social interactions, which we will presuppose in the second half of this study.

Part 1: Prior Concepts

1 *What Is Cybernetics?*

1.1 Initial Concept

Cybernetics is an interdisciplinary approach to organization, irrespective of a system's material realization (Principia Cybernetica Web, Cybernetics); it is derived from *kybernetes*, the Greek word for *steersman*. Heylighen and Joslyn give a very thorough definition (Heylighen and Joslyn, 2001, 2):

> Cybernetics is the science that studies the abstract principles of organization in complex systems. It is concerned not so much with what systems consist of, but how they function ... Being inherently transdisciplinary, cybernetic reasoning can be applied to understand, model and design systems of any kind ...

By its history and content, it can be divided into two: *first-order cybernetics*, which encompasses machines (in the conventional sense of the word) and their study from a detached objective perspective, in which the subject matter can be manipulated at will; and *second-order cybernetics*, which centers on living systems and recognizes that the observed system is an agent that interacts with the observer, and thus has a subjective interactive perspective (Geyer and van der Zouwen).[1]

1.2 History

First-order cybernetics originated when the Josiah Macy Jr. Foundation sponsored a series of interdisciplinary meetings from 1944 to 1953, and reunited noted postwar scholars like Norbert Wiener, John von Neumann, Warren McCulloch, Claude Shannon, Heinz von Foerster, W. Ross Ashby, Arturo Rosenblueth, Gregory Bateson and Margaret Mead (Heylighen and Joslyn, 2001, 2).

Wiener was one of the primary participants of the conferences, as his work on servomechanisms and artillery target mechanisms during World War II sparked his interest in feedback and purpose; in 1948 he published his book *Cybernetics*, in which he summarized the basic principles of the discipline and gave one of the most known definitions (Heylighen and Joslyn, 2001, 2).

As time passed and the objective approach of cybernetics was absorbed by computer science, a focus on autonomy, self-organization, cognition, and the role of the observer in modeling a system consolidated in the 1970s. This became known as second-order cybernetics (Heylighen and Joslyn, 2001, 3).

The distinction between first- and second-order cybernetics was made by Heinz von Foerster in "Cybernetics of Cybernetics", stating that "the cybernetics of observed systems we may consider to be first-order cybernetics; while second-order cybernetics is the cybernetics of observing systems" (von Foerster, 1979, 2).

First-order cybernetics studied systems from a passive and objective perspective, while *the second order recognizes that the observer and the observed cannot be separated, and the observations will depend on their interactions;* this latter approach has become part of the foundations of cybernetics (Heylighen and Joslyn, 2001, 3).

Cybernetics has had a strong influence on the origins of several modern sciences: computer science, information theory, automata theory, artificial intelligence, neural networks, cognitive science, and computer modeling. Most of

---

1 There has been a widespread application of biological cybernetics on social systems; however, this does not constitute an autonomous third order. I have stated the existence of a third- and fourth-order of cybernetics in other works, but to elaborate on them is outside the scope of this study. *See* Roberto Mancilla, *Introduction to Sociocybernetics Part 1: Third order cybernetics and a basic framework for society*, Journal of Sociocybernetics, Vol 9, No 1/2 (2011). https://papiro.unizar.es/ojs/index.php/rc51-jos/article/view/623; Roberto Mancilla, *Introduction to Sociocybernetics Part 2: Power, Culture and Institutions*, Journal of Sociocybernetics, Vol 10, (2012) https://papiro.unizar.es/ojs/index.php/rc51-jos/article/view/625.

its main principles have been assimilated, while some others have been forgotten and are continuously rediscovered, and reinvented in several contexts (Heylighen and Joslyn, 2001, 3).

Cybernetics had its origins in the United States with the Macy Conferences, but also developed in the United Kingdom with Grey Walter and W. Ross Ashby, who can be considered as first-order cyberneticians, and then transitioned to second-order cybernetics by means of the scholarship of Gordon Pask and Stafford Beer (Pickering, 4).

British cybernetics was less about computing and more interested in the study of the human brain. Ashby and Walter were psychiatrists, and the former built a homeostat, a device capable of adapting itself to the environment; the latter built his famous "Turtle", a robot with sensors which exhibited adaptive behavior. Pask centered more on theories of learning and teaching, and his ideas have been rediscovered in other disciplines; Beer applied cybernetics to management and created the Viable System Model, a schema for organizations that is modeled after the human nervous system (Pickering, 2010, 4, 7, and 8).

Cybernetics also developed in the Soviet Union, albeit in a different way. From 1947, when the term *cybernetics* was coined, to 1954, the year after Stalin died, cybernetics was subjected to constant attacks, and with other disciplines it was called a "bourgeois pseudoscience". A decade after this period, it was broadly accepted by scientists, philosophers, and bureaucrats, seen as "the science best fit to build the future Communist society" (Peters, 2012, 145, 146).

By the mid-1960s it was a flourishing discipline in the Soviet Union, but had fallen out of fashion in the United States and England; from this time to the early 1970s, this discipline was normalized into the ideological discourse, and noted practitioners were Alexey Andreevich Lyapunov (1911–1973), Victor Glushkov (1923–1982) and Alexander Yakovlevich Lerner (1913–2004) (Gerovitch, 2002, 4).

Gerovitch analyzed the rise and development of Russian cybernetics over three periods: a) categorical rejection of cybernetics under Joseph Stalin (1948–53); b) embrace of cybernetics as a reformist-oriented science under Nikita Khrushchev (1955–64); c) retooling and diffusion of cybernetics into the service of the status quo and state power under Leonid Brezhnev (1964–80) (Gerovitch, 2002, 4).

1.3 The Scope of Cybernetics

Umpleby compiles a list of definitions of first-order cybernetics, to which Wiener's (Wiener, 11) is added; this item is useful in determining the scope of first-order cybernetics (Umpleby):

Definitions of first-order cybernetics	
von Foerster	The cybernetics of the observed system
Pask	The purpose of a model
Varela	Controlled systems
Wiener	Control and communication in the animal and machine

Varela and Maturana distinguish allopoietic machines from the autopoietic (living systems); the former is defined as "machines that have as a product of their function something different from themselves" (Maturana, Varela, 135). Because they are not the product of their own function, but instead are used for a purpose, *allopoietic machines* (hereafter *machines*) *are controlled systems*.

The notion of machines as controlled systems connects with Wiener, who centers on their control and communication. Now, to control something is to determine its purpose, and therefore, Pask's notion is also addressed. Maturana and Varela coincide with this direction when they say: "Man made machines are all made with some purpose ... This aim usually appears expressed in the product of the operation of the machine, but not necessarily so" (Maturana, Varela, 78).

Because the purpose of the machines is set by their creators and users, it can be said that first-order cybernetics is teleological. It is precisely because of this fact that machines are observed and not observing systems, thus arriving at von Foerster's definition. It can be concluded then that *first-order cybernetics is the study of organization* (observation, communication, and teleology) *in machines that produce things other than themselves and that interact with an observer that studies them or determines their purpose.*

Repeating the method used to ascertain the scope of first-order cybernetics, Umpleby's list of definitions will be used anew to construct a notion of the second order (Umpleby):

Definitions of second-order cybernetics	
von Foerster	The cybernetics of observing systems
Pask	The purpose of a modeler
Varela	Autonomous systems

Maturana and Varela define autonomy as the "self-asserting capacity of living systems to maintain their identity through the active compensation of deformation" (Maturana, Varela, 135). This idea leads to the concept of *autopoiesis*, which is the feature of all living systems, and can be understood as a machine that produces its own components and occupies a space in which it carries out its processes. These types of machines are teleonomical, for they have an apparent purpose or project of organization. If living systems are purposeless in the sense that they are not observed as in the first order, then what is the reason of being of Pask's definition? This is solved by Maturana in his treatment of cognition (Maturana, Varela, 10):

> A cognitive system is a system whose organization defines a domain of interactions in which it can act with relevance to the maintenance of itself, and the process of cognition is the actual (inductive) acting or behaving in the domain. *Living systems are cognitive systems, and living as a process is a process of cognition.* This statement is valid for all organisms, with and without a nervous system.

Because the study of living systems includes cognitive processes, Pask's definition of a modeler applies because a system that observes can determine the purpose of a first-order system that can only be observed; this domain is not entirely exclusive to human beings seeing that there are animals capable of using tools. Second-order cyberneticians acknowledge that no systems can be studied objectively and that the observer plays a crucial role; this means that its definition must have within itself the idea of an observer.

In asking what the properties of the observer are, von Foerster realizes that any observation made entails another act of observation of said observation, and it leads to a problem akin to the Liar's Paradox. To address these deficiencies, he uses Pask's ideas of orders of analysis and concludes that an observer enters the studied system by stipulating its purpose, and by stipulating their own purpose in regards to the observed system. This brings forth Humberto Maturana's famous theorem: "Anything said is said by an observer."

Second-order cybernetics is then the study of observing systems on two levels: first, in the *organization in autopoietic machines*, which are able to build their own components, and possess cognizance which allows them to observe and control other machines; second, in *understanding the derivation of knowledge as a process* in which an autopoietic system observes a system by interacting with it, setting both its purpose and that of the observed. *Second-order cybernetics is a cybernetics of cybernetics.*

1.4 What Is Sociocybernetics?

Sociocybernetics started with the work of Walter Buckley in the late 1960s, which is understood as the application of cybernetics, especially second-order, to sociology (Geyer and van der Zouwen, 2001, 4). As with Luhmann, some sociocyberneticians apply the notion of autopoiesis to social sciences, although there is no joint consensus upon the application of this contested criteria (Geyer and van der Zouwen, 2001, 125). *It has been understood as the application of first- and second-order cybernetics to social systems.*

1.5 What Is Complex Systems Theory?

Complexity theory or studies emerged in 1984, when an interdisciplinary group of 24 scientists met in New Mexico to found the Santa Fe Institute in order to examine complex systems (Santa Fe Institute). These notions originate in the etymology of the word *complexus*, which comes from Latin and means "entwined" or "twisted together". They have continued to gain momentum, spanning to all areas of science, from physics to the natural and social sciences.

However, prior to this, philosopher Edgar Morin attempted to create a transdisciplinary integration of knowledge, which started in *Le Paradigme Perdu* [*Paradigm Lost*], published in 1973, and culminated in his six-volume oeuvre *La Méthode* (1985, 1986, 1991, 1992, 2003, 2006) (Montuori). Prior to these endeavors, transdisciplinarity was attempted by cybernetics, and by general systems theory, a term which was denoted by Bertalanffy in his book *General System Theory: Foundations, Development, Applications* in 1968.

Most of complex systems theory science is prone to taking a first-order approach, as it assumes the perspective of a passive observer – although, as it will be seen, *there are authors* like Robert Northrop *that see it from the second order*. For these reasons, complex systems theory could be understood as a branch or variation of cybernetics.[2]

2 *Recursion, Causality, and Feedback*

Recursion is a type of self-reference, which is a phenomenon that takes place when an idea refers to itself. In computer science, it implies the solving of a problem where the solution is a model of the problem. The latter is summarized in what is known as the Good Regulator Theorem, "Every good regulator of a system must be a model of that system" (Conant, Ashby, 1970), and could easily be visually expressed as the relationship between a lock and a key, the latter containing a model of the former.

---

2 Although many cyberneticians and complexity theorists would contest that notion.

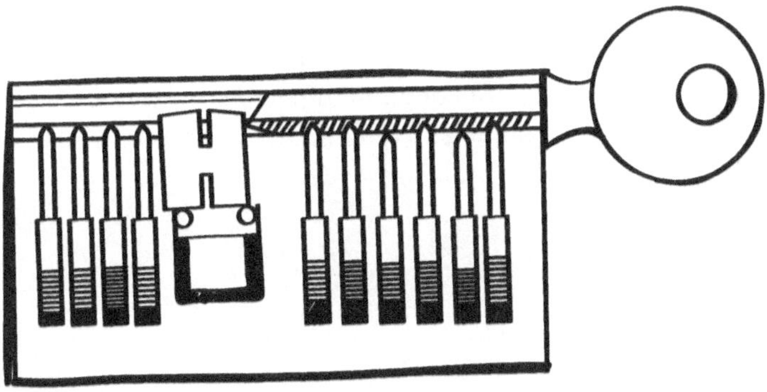

Causality tends to be understood in a linear way when a cause is followed by an effect. However, it can also be understood in a circular fashion: the cause is controlled or affected by its own result (Heylighen, Joslyn, 2001, 10, 11). In information processing systems there are inputs and outputs, in which the former are consequences of the environment's influence on the system, and the latter are the impact of the system on the environment (Principia Cybernetica Web, Feedback Definition). In every feedback loop, information about the result of a transformation or an action is sent back to the input of the system in the form of input data. Feedback can be illustrated in the following manner (Principia Cybernetica Web, Feedback Definition):

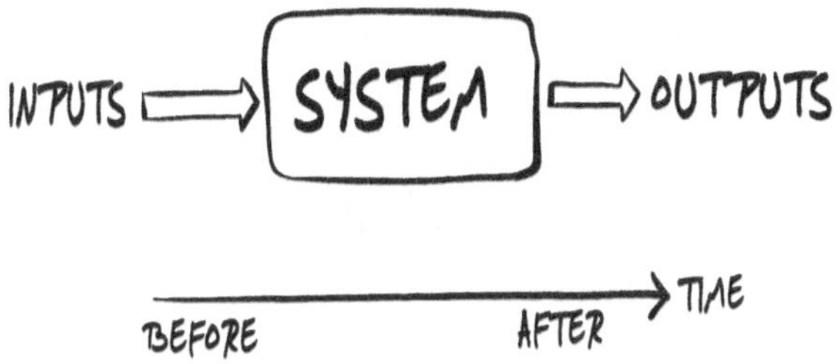

Feedback processes can be of two types: *positive*, when new data allows and accelerates the transformation of input to output in the same direction as the preceding results, thus having cumulative effects and deriving from exponential growth (Principia Cybernetica Web, Feedback Definition); and *negative*, when new data produces a result in the opposite direction to previous ones, stabilizing the system and maintaining an equilibrium (Wiener, 1961, p. 97). These types of feedback can be stated as follows:

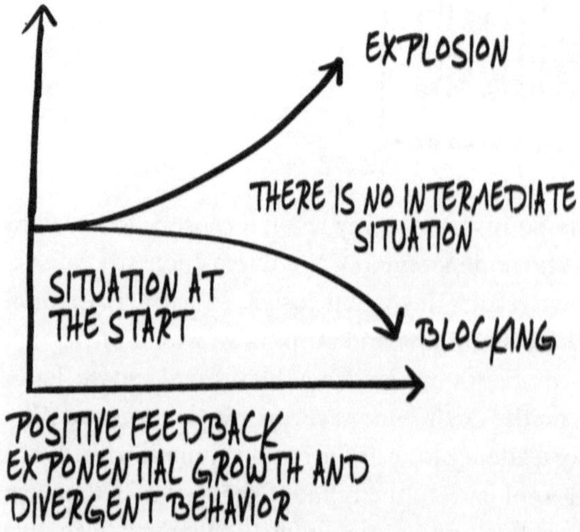

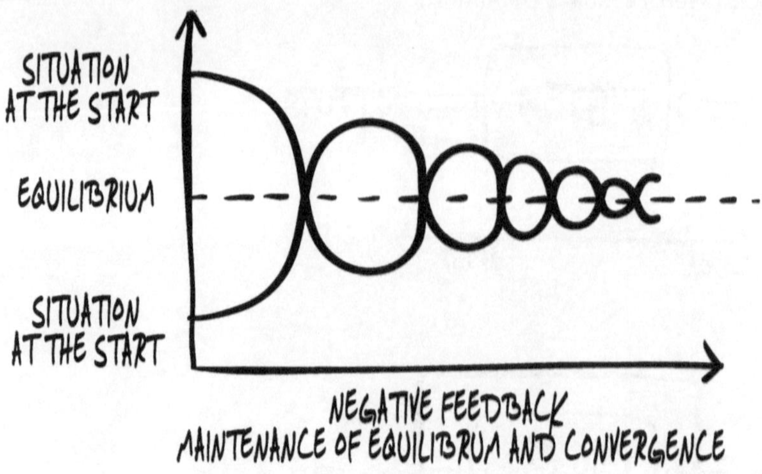

By means of its cumulative effects, a positive feedback left unchecked can lead to the destruction of the system, and this behavior is to be controlled by negative feedback (Wiener, 1961, p. 97). A simple example of a positive feedback is the interest that is accumulated in a bank account, where the money generated reinforces the existing amount; conversely, the regulation of temperature in a body is a mechanism where a successive action counteracts prior ones. All this can be expressed as follows:

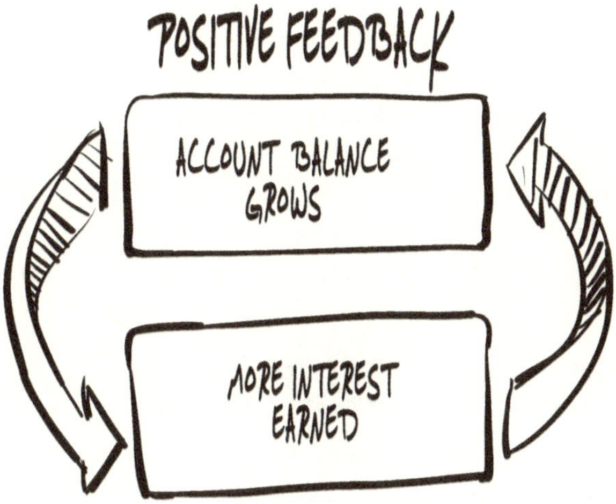

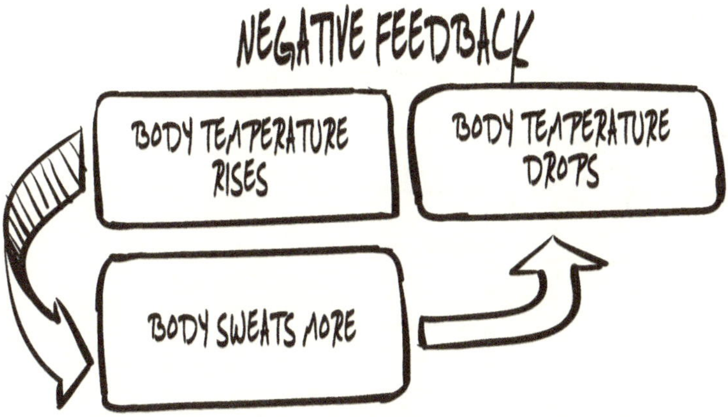

Nature behaves in a circular way: We will see that living systems have elements of self-reference and there are feedback processes between a living system and its environment and with social systems, for the people or animals that comprise it interact with one another and with the environment.

3 *Variety and Self-Organization*

Variety is the set of all possible states that a system can be in and represents the scope that it has in choosing a particular state, and the uncertainty about which state the system occupies. This concept helps us to understand change, choice, and information and thus, how social systems can behave (Principia Cybernetica Web, Law of Requisite Variety).

There is also the *Law of Requisite Variety*, which states that "only variety can destroy variety", that is, when exercising control, the system's capacity cannot exceed its capacity as a channel of communication. This means that there must be a sufficiently large variety of actions or responses to ensure a sufficiently small variety of outcomes; the variety of the system (internal variety) is to be maximized in order to be prepared for any contingency that arises, and the variety of the environment (external variety) can also be reduced (Principia Cybernetica Web, Law of Requisite Variety). All of this can be expressed graphically as follows:

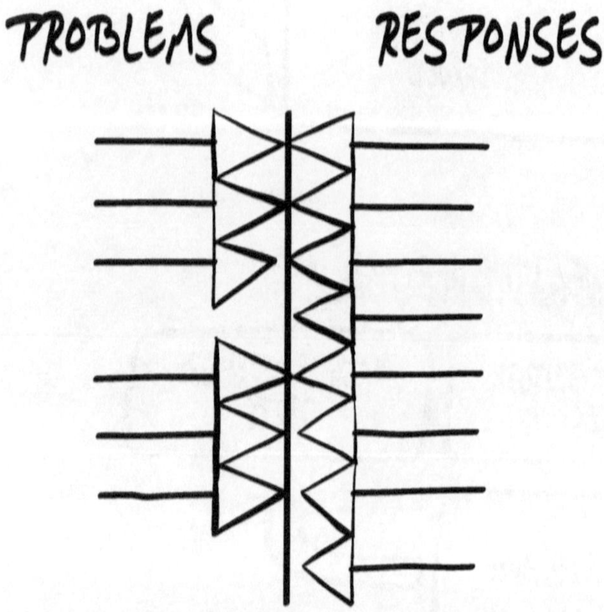

REQUISITE VARIETY: AT LEAST THE RIGHT VARIETY IN RESPONSES TO DEAL WITH VARIETY OF THE PROBLEMS

Self-organization is a phenomenon that arises in living beings and their social systems; a system with known inputs and outputs (like a thermostat) is organized by its user. Self-organizing systems work to maintain themselves, and as they degrade energy as a result, they depend on their surroundings to draw energy and information (Maturana and Varela, 2012, 78,79). They follow cyclical causation: they are both the product and producer of their activity, and through these cycles they define and redefine their boundaries and thus their autonomy (Morin, 2008, pp. 69–70; von Foerster, 2003, p. 3).

In a self-organizing system, there is a "spontaneous emergence of collaborative behavior among elements in a system" at the same time the whole of the system interacts with its environment, and as the system organizes and reorganizes its boundaries as its surroundings change. It also does the same as its own elements develop (Montuori, 2008, p. xxxv).

This whole cycle of organizing and reorganizing of the system and its boundaries in an ongoing interaction can be described by means of two principles: The first – *order from noise* – describes the rise of self-organization as stabilization from states of chaos. The second – *emergence* – describes the advent of new forms from stable behavior. These principles at the same time describe the transition between three states by means of positive and negative feedback: one of a stable equilibrium (*homeostasis*), one of unintelligible information and complete disarray (*hypercomplexity*), and one that mediates between both (*criticality or complex state*).

As a principle of self-organization, the order from noise principle is triggered by internal variation processes referred to as "noise", and it states that random perturbations will help a self-organizing system find more stable states in its fitness landscape. It can be understood as a chain of negative feedback that institutes a spiral causal process in which random configurations of information or chaotic organization stabilize.

This idea was postulated by von Foerster and states that random perturbations will help a self-organizing system find more stable states in its fitness landscape (Principia Cybernetica Web, Order from Noise Principle). The way in which noise is determined is not objective, but rather is made by means of subjective criteria by the observer; when a criterion for relevant information is issued, then one can know what counts as noise. That is, what counts as information and noise are relative to the observer (Ashby, 1965, p. 186).

While the order from noise principle is relative to self-organization,[3] as the attainment of stable states from random perturbations, the emergence principle deals with the rise of unpredictable states or features from seemingly stable states. This type of self-organization is the field of study of dynamical

3 This term is understood both in a physical-chemical sense by Prigogine and a biological sense by von Foerster. See Principia Cybernetica Web, Self-organization, http://pespmc1.vub.ac.be/SELFORG.html.

systems theory, chaos mathematics and complex adaptive systems (Gros, 2008, pp. 35, 40).

Emergent self-organization can arise in systems with many or few variables, but that are sensible to initial conditions; this means that any small change in the initial conditions can make the system grow exponentially or change unpredictably in a short time, which also makes long-term prediction of their output impossible. The example par excellence of this is found in weather prediction (Gros, 2008, p. 40).

Despite this unpredictability there are certain behaviors common to this phenomenon. For example, emergent systems are subject to a series of positive feedback, which develop in a spiral causal process that ends up in exponential growth or organization that renders the output unpredictable on any timescale (short or long).

As was said before, both of these principles operate on the transition of three states. The term *homeostasis* was crafted by American physiologist Walter Cannon in 1932, and is derived from the Greek words *homoios* ("like"), and *stasis* ("to stand"), to mean "to remain the same" or "resistance to change" (Principia Cybernetica Web, Homeostasis); it refers to a state of stability that maintains existing internal balances (Principia Cybernetica Web, Self-organization).

A system of this nature functions on a distinction between itself and the environment, defining its internal organization in relation to everything else that surrounds and interacts with it. Once this is so, the system will deal with the environment in terms of the possible states that the environment can take and it will seek to maintain its identity by means of cyclical causal relations that will augment or diminish its variety and that of its surroundings, in order to achieve stability (Principia Cybernetica Web, Homeostasis).

Dynamic equilibrium is a state of organization that is also known as the "edge of chaos" by those that study complex, chaotic and dynamic systems. Gros defines it as follows: "Self-organized criticality then signifies that the system effectively adapts to changes in the external parameters, e.g. to changes in the given time and length scales, in such a way that the stationary state becomes independent of those changes" (Gros, 2008, pp. 98, 113).

It could be understood colloquially as a stable instability: The system is not completely unstable so as to tear itself apart, but neither is it stable enough to be rigid; it has just the right amount of dynamicity to change and adapt, and the right equilibria to maintain its coherence and structure in the process. This sort of behavior will be shown in systems of all sorts: physical, biological, and social (Gros, 2008, pp. 98, 105).

In *hypercomplexity* there are no objective criteria for determining it; rather, an observer has criteria of it in relation to the activity that is being carried out or regarding the activities of an open system that adapts to its environment.

Relating variety to the states of organization, we can understand the latter in terms of the former: *homeostasis can be a state of low variety*, where the control of possible situations is tenable; *a critical state is one of fluctuating variety* or where there is a greater amount of variety; and the *chaotic state is one of either excessive variety* or one where the fluctuation overcomes the system in perception and capacity for action.

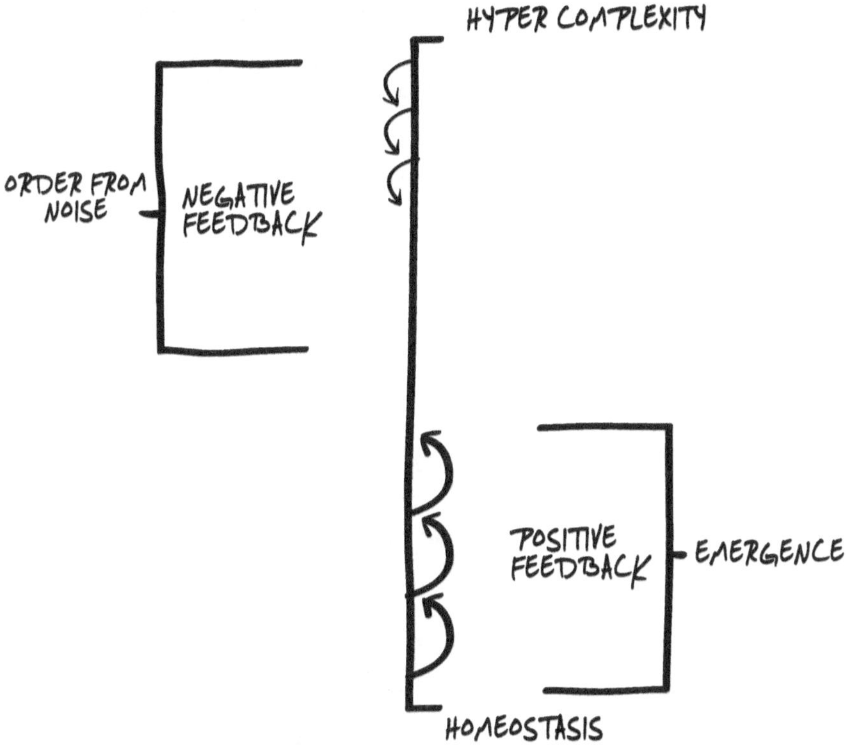

4 *Networks*

A network is a set of relationships between a series of objects (nodes), which is described by an observer. They can start from an organization as simple as a dyad or a triad and are subject to cyclical causality. Networks can be conduits of both wanted and unwanted flows (either unwanted by those that comprise the network or unwanted by the observer who visualizes them) (Kadushin, 2012, pp. 8, 13–14).

A *dyad* can be comprised by nodes 1 and 2 and their interrelation, visualized and understood by the observer; that is, without an observer there is a relationship between the objects, but it is the observer who chooses to understand it as a network. *Triads* further complicate the relation by the addition of a third node, which can lead to 16 different combinations, instead of the binary state of a dyad (there is or there is not). This can be expressed graphically as follows:

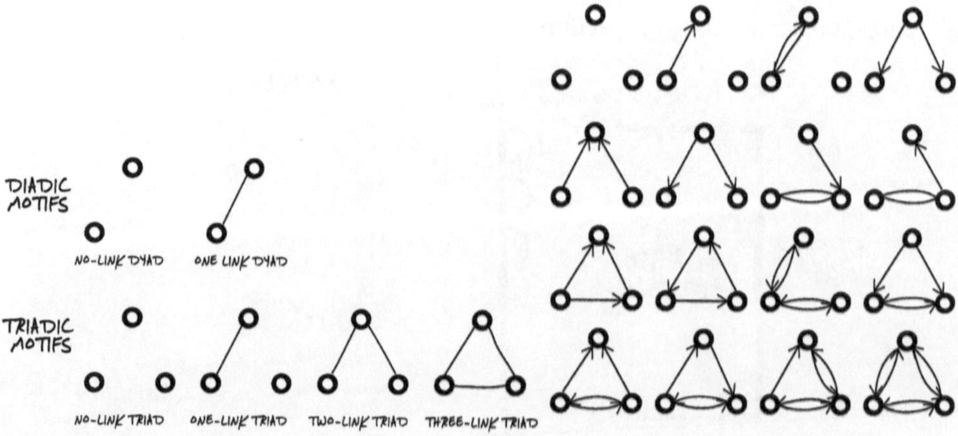

There are *three types of networks*: *ego-centric*, which are those connected by a single node or individual; *socio-centric*, which are relationships within subjects with clearly defined boundaries (closed systems); and *open system networks*, which do not have set limits (Kadushin, 2012, pp. 14, 17). Some examples include:

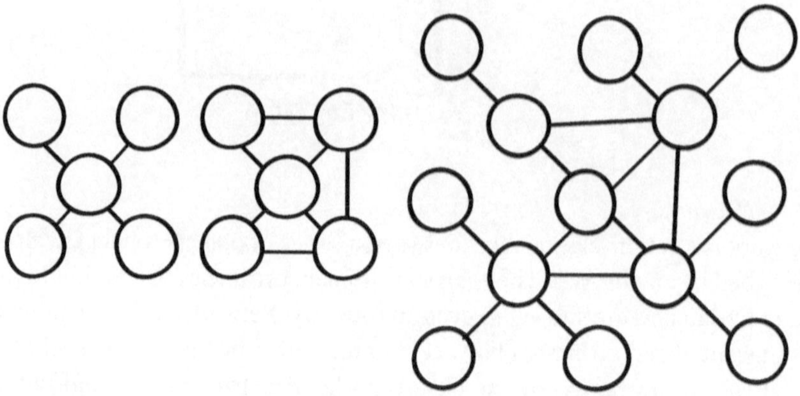

EGO-CENTRIC NETWORK

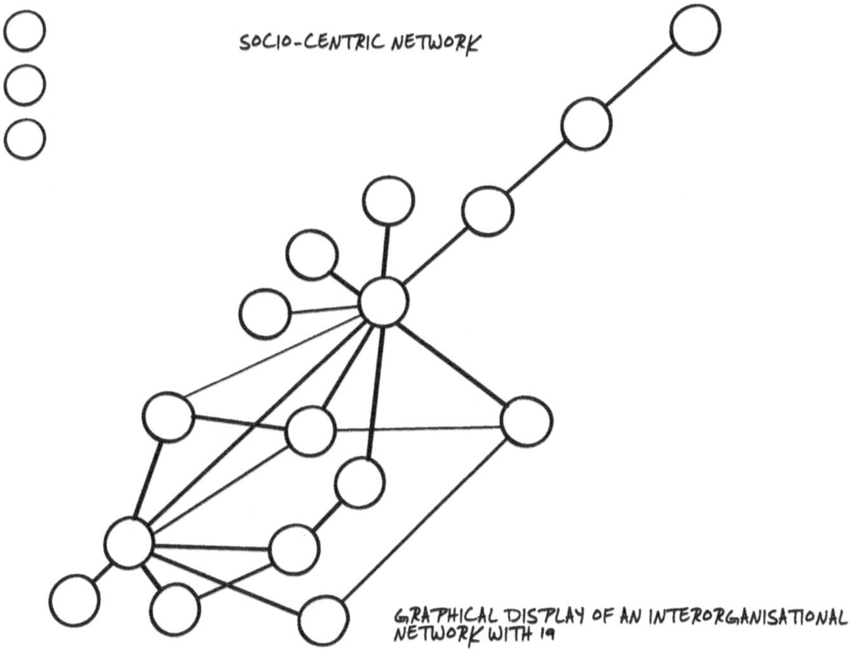

4.1 Socio-centric Network

There are several *features of social networks* that must be taken into account. The first of them is *multiplexity*: social units can have different relationships with others and can overlap and are then connected in varying ways. They can also be visualized by means of graphs and diagrams called sociograms, which can vary in size, organization and purpose according to who makes them; because of their complexity, they are usually created and displayed on computers by means of algorithms and mathematical models (Kadushin, 2012, pp. 202, 203).

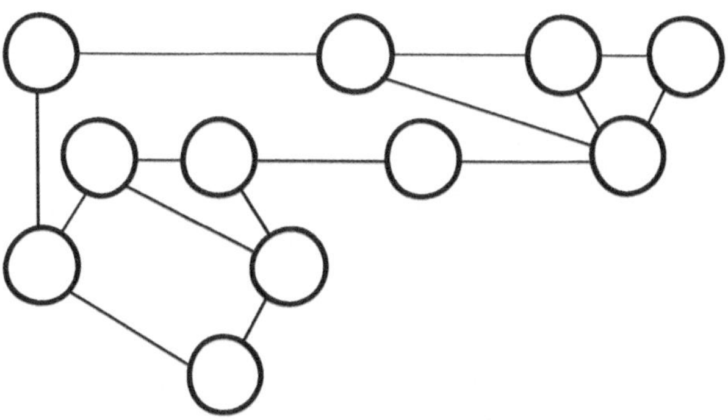

Networks also possess homophily, the tendency of nodes to associate and bond on the basis of a similitude, or simply put, "birds of a feather flock together"; what constitutes similarity and how it is visualized depends largely on the observer. Homophily is a process as well as an outcome. A network can be dense when it possesses a large number of connections between its nodes, which can be related to the motivational need for safety and social support. Alternatively, *a structural hole is the lack of connection between nodes* and can be overcome by certain nodes, which aim to be effective, even though they must go beyond what they consider comfortable. Motivations of safety and effectiveness are present in all social networks (Kadushin, 2012, pp. 204, 205).

A node can have a certain position within a network, which connects them to others and makes them more important as a result; *between-ness* is a measure of position that serves as a bridge, a switching point, or a gateway between different parts of a network, which act as "brokers" because within them one has to pass through to reach other parts (Kadushin, 2012, p. 205). Networks can be used to express hierarchical and heterarchical relations.

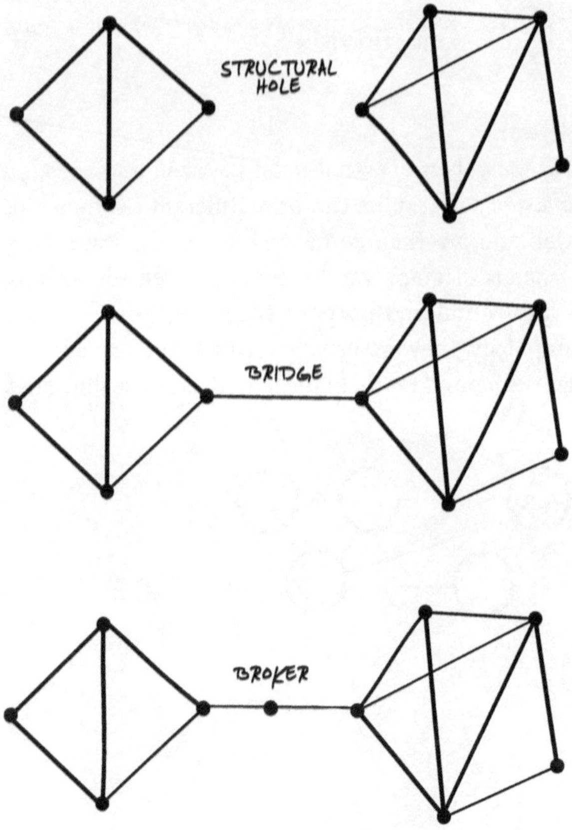

5 *Concepts and Categories*

Concepts are the result of distinguishing a thing from another and giving them a meaning in relation to ourselves or our groups (differentiation and assignation of meaning). Both actions of concept creation are creative in nature: to distinguish is to create a shape and to give meaning is to create content, and these processes, of course, are self-referential in nature.

A *category* can be understood as a grouping of concepts by virtue of a relation that exists between them in accordance to a criterion; that is, they are a set of concepts that share a common property and are put together because of this by a cognizing subject. They are a second-order conceptualization: the grouping of a set of concepts is to be differentiated from others either individually or collectively, and at the same time they have a specific meaning and an internal logic that operates within its elements. For instance:

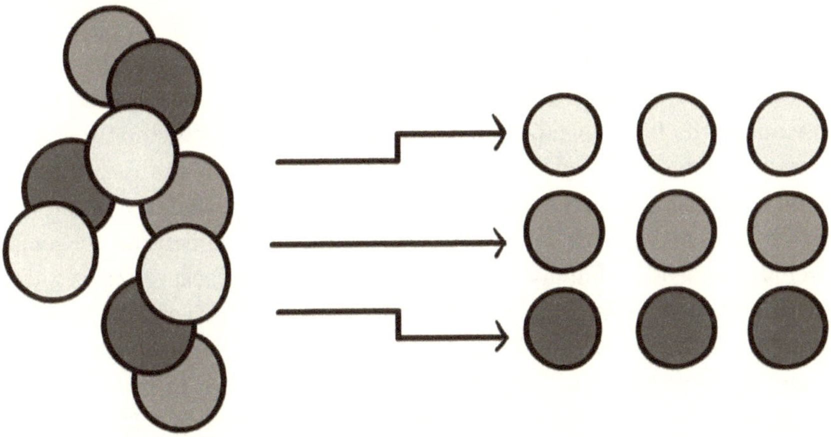

The *relation between concepts and categories is* also *circular*: Categories are concepts, by virtue of reasons previously expounded, but at the same time concepts are subject to being grouped into a category or categories. They are self-referential and subjective because they are established through rules that are crafted in relation to themselves by a subject. A category or concept might be incongruent in relation to a specific concept, but never in relation to itself.

As was discussed in the first part, humans are self-referential, cognizant subjects with an internal dimension that they use as a reference point in dealing with their surroundings, and set what constitutes the boundaries of those surroundings themselves. All social systems are comprised of mutual observation, the recognition of another in relation to the self (Gallese, Keysers and Rizzolatti, 2004). Again:

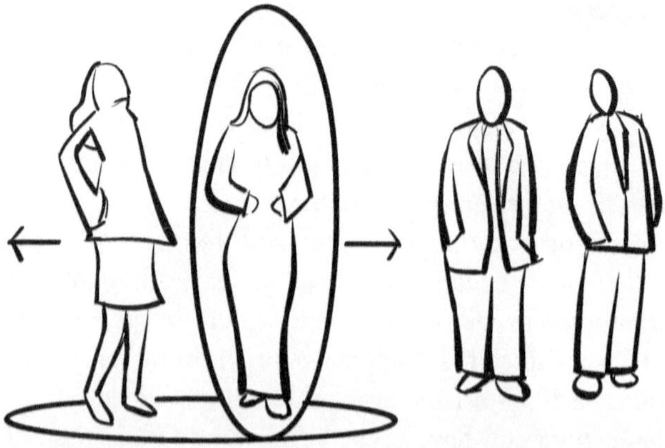

Human sociability, as we know, is the intersection of mutual observation and reflexive observation in relation to a notion of self; that is, self-recognition to its fullest dimension, and the recognition of the other in relation to the former to create a unit that identifies itself as a "we". A social system is a group of individuals who band together for a purpose and share a common frame of reference that is comprised by language and culture (Mancilla 2011; 2012; 2017).

The relationship between humans and social systems is circular: On the one hand, by interacting with their peers in different ways, humans create social systems; on the other, human systems come to be in the background of social systems, culture and language, and thus are "produced" by them. This relation takes place in the backdrop of the repetition of behavior, which is subject to becoming a pattern: Some actions are meaningful enough to be performed again in the future, in the same manner and with the same effort. This involves the narrowing of choice and subsequently involves certainty, as the same problem can elicit the same response (Mancilla, 2017).

Concepts and categories are part of the culture of individuals and are constructed by means of language and communication among individuals. The creation of categories as second-order concepts obeys the necessity of creating frames of reference that help to systemize information into a repository that is accessible to others within a social system. Concepts and categories are a form of discourse created within a social system to systemize information, but at the same time they shape the worldview of humans in their social life. Klare explains as follows (Klare, 1982, p. 1358):

> Legal discourse shapes our beliefs about the experiences and capacities of the human species, our conceptions of justice, freedom and fulfillment, and our visions of the future. It informs our beliefs about how people learn about and treat themselves and others, how we come to hold

> values, and how we might construct the institutions through which we govern ourselves.

Of this I conclude: 1) the public/private distinction is a distinction and meaning assignation made by a group in relation to themselves; 2) it is not universal, but rather is based on an arbitrary distinction; 3) it is a heuristic schema made to systemize and understand existing and incoming information; 4) however, it also molds the worldview of humans, which can be shown merely by pointing out that most Western constitutions incorporate it; 5) it is the product of a specific time and age and is not impervious to changes; and 6) because of its arbitrary roots its ability to change is limited, and it may then be in need of substitution (Mancilla, 2017).

6 *Complexity*

The first thing to know is that there is no widely accepted definition. Heylighen comments as follows on the failure to achieve a definition (Principia Cybernetica Web, What is complexity?):

> The dozens of definitions that have been offered all fall short in one respect or another, classifying something as complex which we intuitively would see as simple, or denying an obviously complex phenomenon the label of complexity. Moreover, these definitions are either only applicable to a very restricted domain, such as computer algorithms or genomes, or so vague as to be almost meaningless.

Despite this, he states that there is a core within all concepts of complexity; a system of this sort requires two or more components joined in such a way that it is difficult to separate them. A system is more complex when a) more parts can be distinguished, and b) more connections between them take place (Principia Cybernetica Web, What is complexity?).

Because complexity has not yet reached a unifying theory regarding its topic of study, there are many varieties of complexity sciences with diverging criteria. Northrop states that there is a wide range of metrics, which include Information, Entropy, Algorithmic Information Content, Fractal Dimension, Excess Entropy, and Metric Entropy, among many others, yet there is no agreement on one that can be applied to all complex phenomena (Northrop, 2010, p. 324). Despite the lack of a general theory of complexity, Geyer and van der Zouwen state four features of complex systems (Geyer, van der Zouwen, 2001, pp. 4–5):

- A system is complex when it is not in a state of either complete order or complete disorder – that is, when it presents a mixture of redundancy and variety.

- Complexity enforces a selective and contingent connection between the system's elements, which always could have been different.
- Complexity is a notion without a difference, without counternotions like transparency or simplicity, and is always bound to an observer.
- A distinction can be made between "simple complexity" and "complex complexity".

Complex systems exist in a state far from equilibrium, between order and chaos (that is, between stability and instability); they cannot be perfectly predicted and can contain subsystems that possess this behavior, and others that can be predicted. Complex systems are then self-organizing in the terms that I stated in this study. Now, Northrop considers complexity in general terms as a "subjective measure of the difficulty in describing and modeling a system (thing or process) and thus being able to predict its behavior" (Northrop, 2010, p. xii).

Much like I did in the third part, he concludes that "Complexity lies in the eye of the beholder: what is complex to one observer may not be complex to another, based on the observer's knowledge and skills". Complexity theorists have strived to achieve a definition that fits all purposes and then debated on the inadequacies of the proposals. In the words of Northrop (Northrop, 2010, p. xii):

> ... it has been very difficult to agree on common, working definitions for complex systems (CSS) and, consequently, to agree on a universal set of quantitative descriptors for their complexity. In fact, universal descriptors may not exist, and probably should not exist. Complexity measures have thus evolved ad hoc for various classes of CSS ...

This means, again, that depending on the system studied, its environment and the qualities of who makes the observation, a system may or may not be considered "complex". Quantitative measurement attempts – the metrics of most of which rely on information theory and use the bit as a measure – ultimately depend on an arbitrary threshold to determine what is complex and compare it between measured systems (Northrop, 2010, p. 323).

Part 2: A Basic Understanding of Human Sociability: The *3 by 3 by 3 Model*

1 *Living Systems*

All social systems are comprised by the living, and thus, to understand how they work, we need to understand the underlying biology. The first thing to note about living systems is that they are non-trivial machines, or in this case, systems; a trivial machine is one where you encounter the same output if you supply the same input. A vending machine is a perfect example – if it takes one dollar to buy a bottle of water, I will always obtain the same output, so long as I provide the same input.

Non-trivial machines are defined by von Foerster as follows: "Their input-output relationship is not invariant, but is determined by the machine's previous output. In other words, its previous steps determine its previous reaction. While these machines are again deterministic systems, for all practical reasons they are unpredictable: an output once observed for a given input will most likely be not the same for the same input given later" (von Foerster, 2003, p. 208).

Non-trivial machines work in cycles because the causes are controlled or affected by their own results (Heylighen, Joslyn, 2001, 12 and 13), and are thus dependent on the past. They are also analytically determinable in their behavior, but unpredictable in their output (von Foerster, 2003, p. 312); that is, you can understand how they behave, but not what they will give as an end result. These types of systems cannot be studied in a reductive way, as they are more than the sum of their parts, and thus they have to be studied as a whole. They also have "inner" states that change with each operation, so an operation is never repeated, but rather other operations will take place (von Foerster, 2003, p. 312).

Non-trivial machines are also open systems, in the thermodynamic sense. Unlike closed systems, where no change is possible because the outputs are always the same and where there is no exchange of information, energy or other states, in this type of system there is an exchange with the environment that is ruled by the laws of thermodynamics (Morin, 2008, p. 22).

Because living systems are non-trivial machines/open systems, they take energy and resources from their environment in order to sustain themselves; however, whereas other trivial and non-trivial machines produce things that are different than themselves, *living systems are autopoietic* (Maturana, Varela, 2012, p. 79),[4] as they produce their own components.

To determine or recast their boundaries, living systems must accumulate energy from their environment to later expend it, which generates entropy and leads to a need for accumulation, in an ongoing cycle; that is, there is a transition from orderly to disorderly states (Morin, 2008, p. 18). Instead of remaining within a single state, living systems then transition constantly from stable to

4 This latter concept was created by Humberto Maturana and then developed with Francisco Varela as a criteria for ascertaining if a system is living or not; these types of systems are closed in the way that they are organized, but they are thermodynamically open.

critical states and depend on their environment to do so; this means that *living systems are organized in a stabilized dynamic.*

Living systems are self-organizing (Morin, 2008, p. 17), for they determine their own purpose by adapting with an environment (Bourgine, Lesne, 2006, pp. 10–11) by means of constant feedback (Brier, 2008, p. 180); this consists not of the suppression of deviations from a goal state, as would happen to a trivial machine such as a thermostat, but rather it is a dynamical process consisting of perceptually guided actions that create a repertoire of actions to be implemented in response to certain stimuli chosen by the system based on a history of interactions with the environment (Varela, Thompson and Rosch, 1993, p. 180).

Self-organization in living systems takes the form of *cognition*, information processing in the form of calculations and logical operations for decision-making, and in the creation of a repertoire of actions; that is, *computation in living systems* – from the smallest to the biggest – *takes place in a self-referential way*, or in the wording of Morin: "computo ergo sum" (Morin, 2008, p. 113; Maturana, Varela, 2012, p. 13).

In computing oneself, living systems posit their identity; the latter is comprised of a notion of "I" as a being animated by its self-organizational subjectivity, and a "me", which can be understood as an objectification of the individual-subject. This allows the system to process its physical body in an objective manner, while remaining a self-organized being; furthermore, cognition and consciousness in living systems are dependent on the computations that their constituent cells have, or "there is no cogito without the computo" (Morin, 2008, pp. 73, 79). Putting all these features together, the following observations can be made:

- The first act of cognition made by an autopoietic is the distinction between itself and its surroundings, which makes the system aware of its surroundings, but also makes it an object of its own observation (Brier, 2008, p. 222). Being a subject is then a fundamental quality of living systems, which cannot be reduced to morphological or psychological singularity (Morin, 2008, p. 77).
- One becomes an observer by "recursively generating representations of our interactions, and by interacting with several representations simultaneously we generate relations with the representations of which we can then interact and repeat this process recursively" (Morin, 2008, p. 14).
- An observer can define itself as an entity by identifying their repertoire of representations, their "cognitive domain"; an organism can achieve self-observation by means of repeated self-description, and self-consciousness by means of self-observation (Maturana, Varela, 2012, 38, 41).

- On the limits of the observer, von Foerster concludes that: "(i) Observations are not absolute but relative to an observer's point of view; (ii) Observations affect the observed so as to obliterate the observer's hope for prediction" (von Foerster, 2003, p. 283).

1.1 Perception

Living beings are in constant communication with the environment that surrounds them. The cognitive function of the observer is as follows (Maturana and Varela, 2012, 8, 9):

> (1) Anything said is said by an observer … (2) The observer beholds simultaneously an entity that he considers (an organism, in our case) and the universe in which it lies (the organism's environment)… (3) It is an attribute of the observer to be able to interact independently with the observed entity from its relations … (4) For the observer an entity is an entity when he can describe it … the observer can describe an entity only if there is at least one other entity from which he can distinguish it, and with which he can observe it to interact or relate … (5) The set of all interactions into which an entity can enter is its domain of interactions. The set of all relations (interactions through the observer) in which an entity can be observed is its domain of relations … (6) The observer can define himself as an entity by specifying his own domain of interactions … (7) The observer is a living system and an understanding of cognition as a biological phenomenon must account for the observer and his role in it.

To act, one must perceive, and that entails sensing and interpreting the ambience of the observer; that is, a domain of interactions and of distinctions presupposes a domain of perceptions, which has a threshold consisting of the minimum amount of stimuli an organ is able to respond to and the maximum amount of stimuli that it is able to interpret coherently. Perception and conceptualizing work in tandem, for what I perceive of the world informs what I know, and vice versa; however, I will treat perception in a separate way.

Perception is the process where all the senses work in tandem to detect and understand objects and the relationship between them, as well as the relationship that they have with the beholder's body. Memory is also important, as past experience of an interaction with an object might help us develop our spatiotemporal skills. For instance, a pitcher has muscle memory and influence determining the way he/she pitches (Oxford University, 2017).

Spatial perception translates into the interplay of skills, such as "locating points in space, determining the orientation of lines and objects, assessing location in depth, appreciating geometric relations between objects, and processing motion, including motion in depth" (Colby, 2001) and which extend to audition and tact and equilibrium (Colby, 2001).

It is also important to note that our senses have a parameter of operations; that is, how much we can perceive (or not) and this enables (and constrains) us in the perception of space and objects. It is also important to realize that while many bind spatial perception to sight, we also construct space by means of what we touch, see, hear, and taste. That is, the perception of space (and also of time) is a full-body experience (Harris et al., 2015).

Our senses, memory and cognition not only permit us to understand the world around us, but by accounting for time, it also allows us to understand how it unravels. That is, without time, we could not interact with the world, and in this, we have to differentiate the time we experience and the time that we measure (Stanford Encyclopedia of Philosophy, Henri Bergson; Stanford Encyclopedia of Philosophy, The Experience and Perception of Time).

Be it that *we can use a measure of time as a reference point for the activities that we can partake in*, or that I have a personal understanding of it that does not need to coincide at times with the measuring of it, time can be understood as a fourth dimension of space that has an observer as a reference point, or as an irreversible progression of events that happen to an observer.

As I said before, our sense of time and space presuppose *memory*, that is, the capacity to remember past experiences in order to make use of them; if we were able to perceive but not remember, we would be unable to interact with the world. Time, space, and memory are nested in one another in the mind of a living system, which is in constant interaction with an environment. Von Foerster says that there are two recurring terms in discussions of memory, which are used interchangeably, but have different natures (von Foerster, 2003, pp. 102–104):

- *Storage and retrieval*: Refers to the storage of documents and signs that do not store information by themselves; rather, such information is constructed or recalled by an observer.
- *Recognition and recall*: Refers to the cognitive process of creating, recognizing, and recalling information from a vehicle that possesses signs.

This means that *with memories, the observer is constructing and reconstructing the information, instead of the information existing in these repositories*; information is observer-based and self-referential as it arises in relation to one who cognizes. This leads us to the conclusion that memory entails a reconstructive process; that is, we never recall the "same" memory twice in the same way. This also entails that there can be false memories or recollections, which can stem from a faulty reconstructive process and lead us to think we have experienced events before (*déjà vu*) or lead us to pass off old memories as new ones (cryptomnesia).

Let us unpack this argument further.

First of all, as was said before, living systems are those that fulfill autopoiesis – that is, that produce their own components, which they do by means of distinguishing themselves from an environment. The creation (and maintenance) of this distinction is self-referential in nature and entails cognition, a series of ongoing computations that are recursive in nature. Memory is what helps to keep the subject-environment distinction through time, as it is the anchor to which the cognizing subject holds on.

Life and cognition are codependent: To live is to compute and to compute is to live. However, both are yoked in subjectivity and the latter at the same time finds its basis in memory, which also at the same time finds its basis in biological processes which give way to cognition. Life/cognition subjectivity and memory all work in a circular dynamic.

Because living systems are thermodynamically open, then, the memory processes that they partake in through their co-enactment with their environment by means of action-perception-cognition are also bound to these laws. That is, memories in a subject are yoked by the laws of physics. Memories are self-referential in nature as well, and because they are bound to cognition, they are part of a constructive/reconstructive process in the way that von Foerster signaled.

1.2 Conceptualizing

The interaction between living systems and their environment is mediated by the information that the former recollect of the latter; such information comes by means of the senses and is constructed by means of the interpretation of stimuli. As reality is experienced by the subject, it is then transformed by them into information; this interpretive activity is constructive in nature, as new meanings may come to be and stored meanings might be revised, and the type of information that a human possesses influences their behavior (Maturana and Varela, 2012, 8, 9).

Kuhn states that concepts are "stored information that things in our environment exist in certain patterns, but not others" (Kuhn, 1963, p. 28). This may have the following limits: (1) concepts correspond to things which are associated in the environment; (2) things cannot be perceived until concepts of them are formed; (3) there can be concepts of objects (static things) and events (dynamic things); and (4) while there can be concepts of wholes as consisting of certain parts, concepts of parts belonging to certain wholes are also formed (Kuhn, 1963, pp. 29–30).

Perception and conceptualization have a circular relation: Sensory input brings forth the possibility of new signals from which new concepts can be constructed in order to understand them, but at the same time, new concepts determine the way in which sensory input is to be interpreted.

A useful point of departure in expounding what conceptualizing is lies in the concept of information as interpreted by Gregory Bateson: "the difference that makes a difference" (Bateson, 2000, 462). Ashby coincides with the importance of difference, although he does not equate it to information. He says: "The most fundamental concept in cybernetics is that of 'difference', either that two things are recognizably different or that one thing has changed with time" (Ashby, 1965, p. 9).

To create a concept entails the differentiation of one thing from another, and that process has three elements: a pattern, a proportion, and a viable combination of both. The *Oxford English Dictionary* defines *order* as "the arrangement or disposition of people or things in relation to each other according to a particular sequence, pattern, or method" (Oxford Dictionary, Order) and *pattern* as "a regular and intelligible form or sequence discernible in the way in which something happens or is done" (Oxford Dictionary, Pattern).

The following elements can be extracted from these definitions: a) ordered entities (people or things), b) a rule or pattern under which the objects are arranged, and c) a relationship between the ordered objects. Furthermore, if the self-referential nature of cognition is taken into consideration, then other elements are to be added: d) the existence of an orderer, which comprises both organization and self-organization; e) the relation between the ordered and ordering agent, f) the relation between the ordered and the rule, and g) the goal pursued by the balancing agent (Mancilla, 2013, 54).

Balance can be understood as "a condition in which different elements are equal or in the correct proportions" (Oxford Dictionary, Balance); *proportion* is also defined as "a part, share, or number considered in comparative relation to a whole" (Oxford Dictionary, Proportion). These ideas presuppose by analogy the same elements as those of the pattern/order (Mancilla, 2013, 56–58).

The mediation between patterns and proportion brings forth a third idea which I will call *harmony* and which can be defined as the conjunction between order and balance in a compatible relation. Patterns and proportions cannot function without each other, and along with harmony, they have a triadic recursive relation: to stand by themselves, the pattern, the proportion, and their implementation presuppose within themselves a pattern, a proportion and a viable implementation. That is, the elements of differentiation are a differentiation in and of themselves (Mancilla, 2013, 61).

Semiotics concerns itself with the study of signs in the broadest of senses, which are not to be analyzed as isolated phenomena, but studied in relation to how meaning is constructed and reality is represented. I will make use of Peircean semiotics, which conceives of signs as an irreducible triad. To him, *a sign* "is something which stands to somebody for something in some respect or capacity" (Feibleman, 1970, p. 88); that is, *it is a reference frame by means of which a cognitive system can give a value or a meaning to something, having differentiated it from other things.*

To Peirce, semiotics is the equivalent of logic, the latter which he defines as "the science of the general necessary laws of signs ... only another name of semiotic, the quasi-necessary, or formal doctrine of signs" (Feibleman, 1970, p. 88). This means that Semiotics or Logic is the study of the rules of the appropriate meaning assignation to a differentiated object in order to use it as a reference, which is subsumed into a repertoire of signs that make up the knowledge and experience of the cognizing subject; *knowledge and experiences are then sign-based and are subject to construction and reconstruction.*

To Peirce, the signs have the following elements: *representamen*, the form which the sign takes; *interpretant*, the sense made of the sign; and *object*, something beyond the sign to which it refers. The interrelation between the elements of the sign is called *semiosis* by Peirce, and is a product of observation, as signs are created by the cognizing subject and then submitted to an existing repertoire; they are then also a product of self-observation (Feibleman, 1970, p. 89). Signs can be visualized in the following way (Chandler, 2007, p. 30):

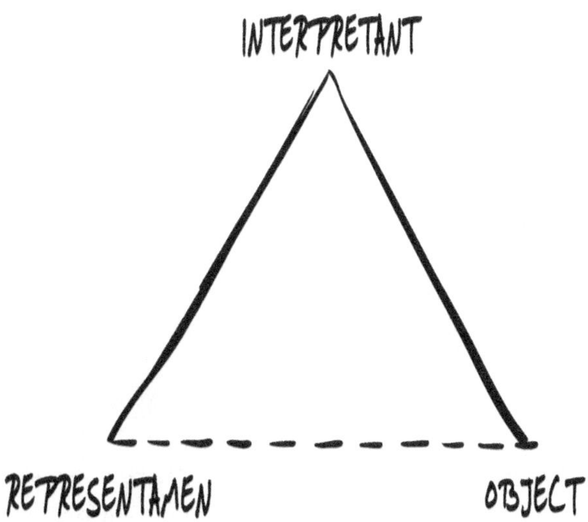

To exist, a sign must fulfill the following conditions: it must correlate with or represent an object (representative condition); it must represent or correlate with that object in some respect or capacity (presentative condition); the sign must determine an interpretant (interpretative condition); and the relation between sign, object and interpretant must be triadic (triadic condition) (Liska, 1996, p. 19).

Signs have no final object, because an object can be another sign, and so on, or as he states in his principle, "a sign is something by knowing which we know something more"; also, they are context-dependent, and cannot exist in isolation (Eco, p. 2). This has as a consequence a circular causation process that leads to an infinite process of interpretation, which can be stated in two ways: 1) the object of a sign can be another sign, and 2) the interpretant is nothing but a representation, which as such has an interpretant (Brier, 2008, pp. 98, 114; Chandler, 2007, p. 32).

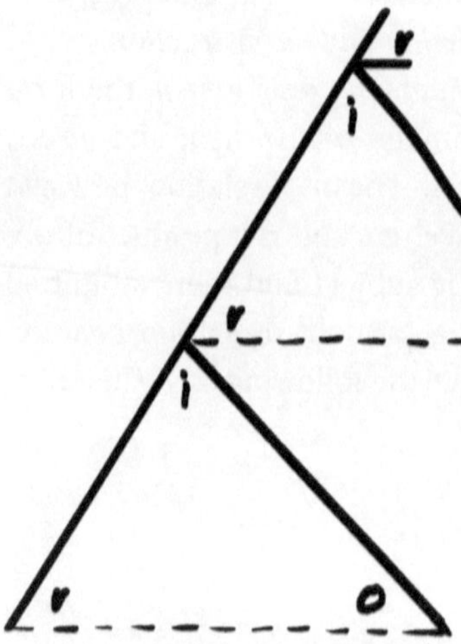

As reality is experienced by the subject, it is then transformed by him into signs using semiosis. This entails an interaction between external and internal factors: signs can be things from the outside, but an observer can also define themself by means of signs. Therefore, *the usefulness of signs lies in their power to determine the possibilities of how the observers interpret signs in their future activity* (Brier, 2008, p. 270).

Sign processing provides the observer with a point of contact with the environment, be it a physical one, or other observers as a social system. On its most basic level, *everything that the observer experiences, understands and conceives, he does so in reference to his own body.* Body language, gestures and noises can create a cooperative domain of interactions between subjects through the development of a common frame of reference, although each of them acts exclusively within his cognition (Maturana, Varela, 2012, p. 57).

This constitutes what Varela et al. call the embodied approach, which emphasizes that sensory and motor processes are inseparable in living cognition as they have coevolved together. In it, cognition depends upon the experience that comes from having a body with various sensorimotor capacities; perception consists in perceptually guided action (Varela, Thompson and Rosch, 1993, pp. 172–174, 176).

Cognitive structures emerge from the recurrent sensorimotor patterns that enable action to be perceptually guided, but individual sensorimotor capacities are themselves embedded in a more encompassing biological and psychological context. The organism chooses the stimuli in the physical world to which it will be sensitive in order to survive; this is accomplished by categorization and the uniqueness of each experience is transformed into a set of learned, meaningful categories to which the organism responds (Varela, Thompson and Rosch, pp. 172–174, 176).

The basic level of conceptualization is the point where cognition and environment become simultaneously enacted; as environment and organism interact, they coevolve with each other through their history of interactions, which Maturana and Varela have called *structural coupling*. Varela puts forth as an example of this the coevolution of the color of flowers, on par with the ultraviolet-sensitive, trichromatic vision of bees (Varela, Thompson and Rosch, pp. 177, 201). Cognitive capacities are then inextricably linked to histories that are lived, unlike the traditional view of cognition as problem-solving on the basis of representations (Varela, Thompson and Rosch, 1993, p. 205).

1.3 Consciousness as the Coordination of Information into a Subjective Perspective

One of the shortcomings of Maturana and Varela, on their positions on autopoiesis and cognition, is that they presuppose the existence of consciousness – that is, internal qualitative subjective states. In a basic sense, this is a state of states of sentience and awareness that consists of the unification of the existing information that different mechanisms in the brain utilize to perceive the surroundings of the subject. To develop this point, it is necessary to explain brain functions in living systems.

A neuron is a cell which processes and transmits information through electrical and chemical signals with other alike cells by means of specialized connections called synapses, and they can link with each other and form networks. It has the following components: soma, dendrites, and an axon (University of Washington).

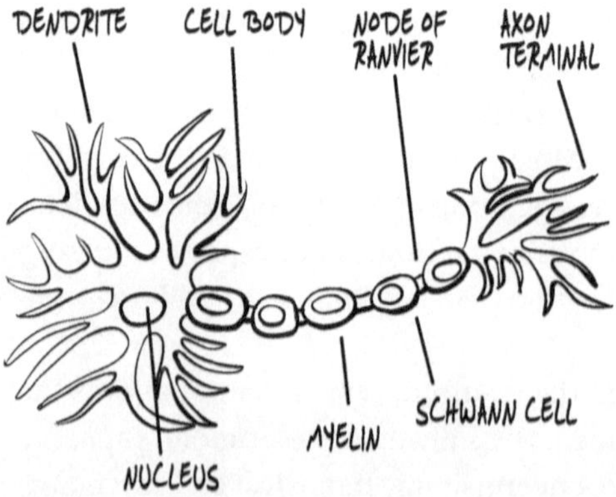

The soma is bulbous, while the dendrites and axon are filaments that emanate from it; the former branch profusely, getting thinner with each branching, while the latter leaves the soma at a swelling called the axon hillock, and can extend to great lengths. Neural function is realized by the synaptic signaling process, which is partly electrical and partly chemical; these types of signals are transmitted by the axon and received by the soma and dendrites. Synaptic signals are excitatory when they make a neuron likely to fire a nerve impulse or act on potential, and inhibitory when the affected neuron has the opposite action (University of Washington).

Von Foerster states that neural machinery is functionally organized to establish, from sensory information, relations between observed systems and the system that makes the observation, which at the same time can modify the latter's behavior on the basis of existing information (be it of the external world or of internal states). This he takes to be the minimal case of a cognitive process, and he defines it as a "Cognitive Tile" (von Foerster, 2003, p. 119).

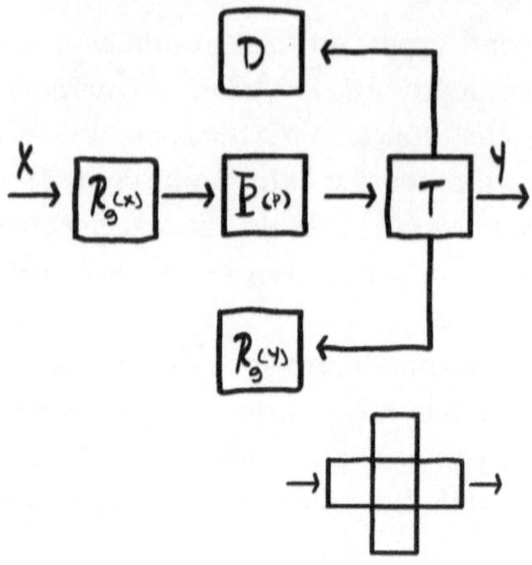

A cognitive tile is a simplification of a cognitive process, or an aggregate of simple processors (in this case, neurons). The left side of the tile represents perception, self-referential relations in the spatiotemporal configurations of stimuli and responses; the right side comprises what he calls element *T*, which translates the output into a universal "internal language" which other tiles can use; the top part has a delay loop that operates on the feedback that comes from the output, while the bottom has one loop that processes all the relational information of the system's actions in accordance with its goals. At the center of the cross, there is a finite function machine – an abstract machine that can find itself within a finite function of states, although only one at a time – that changes states according to the quantifications of the tile (von Foerster, 2003, pp. 119–121).

Tiles may assemble with one another in order to form a tessellation and operate as a *heterarchy*, a non-hierarchical organization where they can be organized in different ways as circumstances demand. In the words of von Foerster (von Foerster, 2003, p. 123):

> When in operation, this system shifts kaleidoscopically from one particular configuration of cooperating sets of adjacent tiles to other configurations, in an ever changing dynamic mode, giving the impression of "clouds" of activity shifting, disappearing and reforming as the task may demand.

One can take this idea of a tessellation and state that this process gives way to yet another mechanism – which I have called, in previous scholarship, *cognitive machines* – which can process information in general, but also has specialized routines and functions that determine its identity, and has a type of working memory that allows it to account for previous behavior. This seems to hold some water, for Stillings et al. – referring to human cognition – state the nature of the cognitive architecture of living systems as follows (Stillings et al, 1995, p. 16):

> The high degree of flexibility of human cognition requires that we think of much of the human cognitive architecture not as determining specific thoughts and behaviors but as an abstract set of mechanisms that potentiates a vast range of capabilities.

Because *Consciousness is the unification of information in a self-referential process*, its first component is a basic sense of identity that begins with *self-computation, which integrates the "I" as subjective experience and the "me" as the objectification of the subject into the self*; at the same time, identity influences consciousness as it functions as its frame of reference.

Regarding the scope of the subjective, Morin enunciates two principles that are useful for this task. One is called the *exclusion principle* and means that only the observer can say "I" for himself, that is, only he is capable of self-reference. The "I" is something banal and unique at the same time. The other is the *inclusion principle*, which states that a plurality of "I" can be integrated into a "we" (Morin, 2008, p. 75).

Ned Block makes a distinction between *Access-consciousness, or A-consciousness*, a state where information is ready for a cognizing subject to use, that is, information can be used and retrieved by means of introspection, for verbal communication, deliberation and self-control; and *Phenomenal-consciousness, or P-consciousness*, which consists of the experiential states that the cognitive system has. A state is P-conscious if it has experiential properties, and the totality of the experiential properties of a state are "what it is like" to have it. It cannot be defined in a non-circular way (Block).

The interplay between A- and P-consciousness can be understood as a state of awareness and consists of a mechanism that allows the coordination of all cognitive machines and their independent information processing; that is, it is a "cross-talk" mechanism (Morsella, Jantz, 2011, pp. 83, 85). Morsella and Jantz state that because there are many quasi-independent computers in the brain (cognitive machines, in our terms), which can perform several complicated actions and influence action in general, consciousness acts as a Wi-Fi system to integrate the different processes in the brain and give way to adaptive action (Morsella, Jantz, 2011, p. 88).

Shevrin resonates with this and defines consciousness as an irreducible experience associated with different psychological states, but is not to be confounded with the latter's functions. Both definitions are correct, but they grasp different aspects: While Morsella and Jantz comprise the biological aspects of consciousness as a cognitive machine, that is, the "hardware", Shevrin touches more on the information processing aspects, the "software" (Shevrin, 2011, p. 186).

An important aspect of cognitive machines is that because each of them are functionally specialized to perform different functions, they entail different types of sign processing, and thus speak different "languages", which consciousness in its coordinating function must interpret and translate, with the risk of some information ending up lost in translation (Joseph, 2011, p. 344).

In conclusion, Consciousness can be understood as the interplay of four different cognitive mechanisms: one which unifies all the input of other cognitive machines (Phenomenal-consciousness), another that makes said information retrievable in introspection (Access-consciousness), another which ensures the coherence of existing information processing by uniting it into a single viewpoint (Identity) and another that comprises the means of transmission of the existing information to other cognitive systems (sign processing).

2 *How Does This Relate to the Social?*

This recursive triad summarizes the basic behavior of those subjects that can integrate a social system, human or otherwise. That is, these are the basic cognitive foundations of social behavior, which takes place by means of sign processing – both in language and face-to-face communication – and of human cognition, which takes self-reference to a deeper level.

In this basic sense, living systems are bodies that adapt by means of perceiving stimuli, creating concepts of what they grasp and computing themselves in relation to their environment – creating, in the process, a basic sense of identity. It will be seen later that this self-referential behavior (von Foerster, 1979, 1) permeates human sociability on two sides: firstly as mutual observation by cognizing subjects that conceive themselves as an entity (a "we") (Mancilla, 2011, 41, 42) and secondly as reflexive observation, the tension between being a body and having a body (Mancilla, 2013, 50).

3 *Human Cognition*

Briefly reprising what was said about living systems, Maturana gives the following treatment of cognition: "A cognitive system is a system whose organization defines a domain of interactions in which it can act with relevance to the maintenance of itself ... Living systems are cognitive systems, and living as a process is a process of cognition. This statement is valid for all organisms, with or without a nervous system" (Maturana, Varela, 2012, p. 13). Von Foerster adds that cognition is equal to computing a reality; in the most general sense, computation is a mechanism for ordering, which can take place on two levels: 1) when we wish to make a description of a given arrangement of things; and 2) when we wish to rearrange things according to a certain description (von Foerster, 2003, p. 194).

This notion of computation brings forth a tension between what the observer perceives and what he knows, for the first one entails the creation of knowledge according to perception and the second one the recasting of perception according to existing concepts. This leads to the notion of "Cognition computing descriptions of a reality".

Knowing this, how is human cognition distinguished from that of living systems? Despite both being capable of being self-referential by virtue of their recursive computations, reflexive observation has proven to be something exclusive to human beings, which is the only species capable of self-face recognition, which has been used as a measure of higher-order self-processing as the self-face is the most obvious embodied representation of the self (Uddin, Iacoboni and Keenan, 2007). Berger and Luckmann perfect this observation (Berger and Luckman, 1967, p. 50):

> On the one hand, man is a body, in the same way that this may be said of every other animal organism. On the other hand, man *has* a body. That is, man experiences himself as an entity that is not identical with his body, but that, on the contrary, has a body at its disposal ... man's experience of himself always hovers in a balance between being and having a body, a balance that must be redressed again and again.

In his widely known psychological research, Piaget makes a typology of the cognitive development of a human being from its birth to adulthood, in which every state is distinguished from its preceding one because of the appearance of new original cognitive structures. In this typology, the difference between lower and higher cognition can be seen more clearly: While in the sensorimotor there is motor activity, knowledge based on experience and interaction and limited language acquisition, in the formal operational stage an individual can communicate to others by means of a symbol system and is capable of logical and abstract reasoning (Piaget, 1974, pp. 14–15).

Brier notes that both animals and humans live in self-organized fields or repertoires of representations (which to us are differentiated objects with a meaning assigned to them), which they project around themselves and deep inside their systems (Brier, 2008, p. 100); cognition and structural coupling with the environment allow the creation of habits that create these fields, and organize the meaning that the system gives to its surroundings and to itself in relation with everything else.

Internal mental organization is projected towards the exterior by means of action and is a product of constant perceptual feedback; in animal cognition this is represented in what Brier calls "sign games", and in human cognition, it is represented by means of language and social self-conscious signification, or in Wittgenstein's terms, "language games" (Brier, 2008, p. 234). As to the goal-directedness of human cognition, like all living systems, human beings interact with an environment in order to obtain resources and energy from it for self-sustainment; however, they can also determine goals of their own due to reflection and self-observation, which, as was said before, serve as the point of transition between animal and human cognition.

3.1 Experiential Cognition

To me, experiential cognition is a type of cognition made without taking the sequential steps of logical cognition, and is used to derive knowledge and interact with the environment. Wiener foresaw other types of cognition when he said that there are psychological states and sequences of thought that do not conform to logic (Wiener, 1961, p. 125). This type of cognition builds upon the embodied and perceptual aspects of the cognition general to all living systems and takes it further into the reflexive dimensions that are proper to human thought.[5]

We have stated the importance of perception, as it is the identification and processing of sensory information which gives input to cognition and which at the same time is built upon it. Although perception has been accounted for already, it is necessary to see how it changes with the reflexivity that human beings possess.

In human beings, perception comprises three aspects: On the one hand, *perception is a vital input in the construction of reality*, as it was understood with spatial and temporal perception as an embodied activity and memory. Human beings, as it was said, possess a more profound dimension of the self that entails being in a body and having it at one's disposal, and this is reflected in the fact that to construct the idea of a body, we have to perceive it first. The way in which we construct a notion of self-reference, which anchors our relation to an environment, requires a perceptual input. That is, perception helps us to *construct the self.*

5 I have laid the framework for the study of reflexivity in my paper "Introduction to Sociocybernetics (Part 3): Fourth Order Cybernetics", published in the Journal of Sociocybernetics.

Perception[6] also partakes in the construction of the social, as several notions of the "I" can be used to create a "we" and humans as social beings help build the collective, but at the same time, they are shaped by it. It is a coevolutive process. That is, we build and are built by the society we form and perception is a central part in such endeavors.[7] For instance, infrastructure has been designed largely for the able-bodied, and only recently have ideas like universal access and design been taken into policy.

One interesting pair of hypotheticals that might explain the relationship between perception and the construction of reality, the self and the social is this: Imagine that a man from 15th-century Europe is transported to any city in the 21st century. He discovers cars, airplanes, and electricity, which are things outside his worldview; his perception is partly anchored in his social context and thus, *what he perceives is informed by his conception of the world.*

Conversely, imagine that humans are born blind and thus, the notions of physics that they have would be different from that of our humankind; or maybe they would differ from those of another version of our species bestowed with the complex eyesight of a mantis shrimp, an animal capable of perceiving wavelengths of light that include deep ultraviolet, far-red and polarized light. Thus, *what we perceive also informs what we construct.*

Within experiential cognition, we also find *intuition, or non-logical cognition,* which has been studied by philosopher Henri Bergson. He criticizes Intelligence by stating that it is guided by needs and thus generates relative knowledge, with the method being used to divide things according to a particular perspective. Intuitive or non-logical cognition in its processes and workings reverses Intelligence by deriving knowledge from experience and feeling instead of creating a differentiation and synthesis of viewpoints (Stanford Encyclopedia of Philosophy, Henri Bergson).

All this has been exemplified by Daniel Kahneman in his book *Thinking, Fast and Slow,* where he states that the human mind is divided into two systems that work together: 1, which operates automatically, without effort and

6 Despite the fact that Maturana, Varela and von Foerster treat cognition as something that can't be separated, when the first two talk about the domain of "representations" and of "discourse", cognition and sign-making are separated; this too could be done with perception, as changes in the latter affect the living system's capability of forming representations and of communicating. What we perceive, cognize and communicate are intertwined and we lose information if we ignore one of the three.

7 As we construct concepts, we also construct the idea of ourselves and others. Bernard Scott makes an excellent summary of how cybernetics has developed regarding the idea of the construction of the self – both as self-awareness and reflection – by means of social processes mediated by languages; see "The Co-Emergence of Parts and Wholes in Psychological Individuation", published in *Constructivist Foundations* in March of 2007.

sense of control, and 2, which operates on effortful mental operations and encompasses self-control. System 1 can operate automatically complex patterns of ideas, while System 2 constructs thoughts in an orderly way. These systems are geared towards minimizing effort and maximizing performance (Kahneman, 2011, pp. 20–21, 25).

Like Kahneman, Bergson also concludes that Intelligence (System 2) is conscious and instinct is unconscious (System 1), and also, although they are complements, they exclude each other. He also distinguishes degrees of knowledge instead of types: "knowledge that is acted and unconscious is instinctive, while the one that is thought and conscious is intelligent" (Kahneman, 2011, p. 149). In this tenor of things, instinctive knowledge resembles categorical propositions while intelligent knowledge is expressed hypothetically.

The subjective experience of emotion and how it permeates into the social is another important but grossly overlooked factor in the cognition that is experienced and felt (and also, in general, in the study of human behavior). *Emotion* is usually viewed as a nuisance or as a distortion within rational decision-making (Bandes, Blumenthal, 2012), but it *colors the way we conceive, experience and interact with the world* – second-order cybernetics shows us that living beings, and humans with them, are subjective, but in my perspective, the latter are also emotional beings.

Regarding the social level, there are aspects that need to be taken into account: a) emotion influences the implementation of norms and policy; b) emotion can be channeled to influence decision-making; and c) emotions are not a purely individual and internal phenomenon, but rather can be channeled (as a "we") and thus are an important component of social and institutional dynamics (Bandes, Blumenthal, 2012).

Human beings are not rational decision-makers, because we have intuitive and emotional processes that partake in what I will define as logical cognition – and this is not a bad thing. These felt aspects of human cognition have been ignored and underplayed by social scientists, but they are important in understanding the social.

3.2 Logical Cognition

Logical cognition is a set of sequential steps that is formed by two or more judgments, ordered in a way such that the latter can be inferred from the former; it implies a mediate relationship between concepts and an immediate relationship between judgments, and is a reference to objects. Knowledge generated by means of a reasoning is discursive knowledge; the one generated by means of an immediate grasping of an object (that is, without reasoning) is intuitive knowledge. These types of knowledge are complementary, for they support each other – discursive knowledge is ultimately based on intuitive, and the latter's validity is proved by the former. *Logical cognition is comprised by reasoning, which can be classified by the relationship between premises and conclusions into the deductive, inductive and abductive.* (Brier, 2008, pp. 215–217).

Deduction is "an argument whose interpretant represents that it belongs to a general class of possible arguments precisely analogous which are such that in the long run of experience the greater part of those whose premises are true will have true conclusions" (Feibleman, 1970, pp. 116, 119, 121). In deductive reasoning the premises are claimed to support the conclusion in such a way that it is impossible for the premises to be true and the conclusion false, and consists of the application of general rules to particular cases. It begins from a hypothetical state of affairs abstracted from data, and is independent from the latter (Walton, 2004, pp. 2, 8, 10, 12–13).

Induction is the argument which proceeds upon the assumption that all the members of a class or aggregate have all the characters which are common to all those members of this class concerning which it is known, whether they have these characters or not (Feibleman, 1970, pp. 116, 119, 121). In inductive reasoning the premises are claimed to support the conclusion, so it is improbable that the premises be true and the conclusion false; it consists in departing from a theory, inferring from it predictions of phenomena and observing them to see how much it coincides with the point of departure. This type of inference goes from the case and the result to the rule; like deduction, it takes data as a basis, and partially extrapolates beyond it (Walton, 2004, pp. 2, 8, 10, 12–13).

Abduction is an argument which presents facts in its premise which bear a similarity to the fact stated in the conclusion, but which could perfectly well be true without the latter being so … and thus we are not led to assert the conclusion positively but are only inclined toward admitting it as representing a fact of which the facts of the premise constitute an icon (Feibleman, 1970, pp. 116, 119, 121).

To me, abduction is more related to feeling or qualia, than reaction or habit-making; this is so because in this type of inference it is implausible that the premises are true and the conclusion false. It is the weakest of the three kinds, as an abductive conclusion is essentially an intelligent guess.

It is also known as inference to the best explanation, as it consists of reasoning from given data to a hypothesis that explains it. Unlike deduction and induction, which depart from the general to the particular, and the particular to the general, respectively, abduction departs from particular to particular, and is often associated with the kind of reasoning used in the construction of hypotheses in the discovery stage of scientific evidence (Walton, 2004, pp. xiii, 2, 3, 4).

Meditating on the reaches and nature of intellect, Bergson concludes that the human intellect thinks in terms of solids and inanimate objects, which ends up being an imitation of life and of experienced knowledge; thus, for this author, logical cognition is a static version of experienced cognition. Furthermore, intellect is fashioned after the needs of human action, thus proceeding by calculation, adapting means to ends and by thinking out mechanisms of geometrical form (Bergson, 1920, pp. ix, 4, 47).

Bergson defines Intelligence as "the faculty of manufacturing artificial objects, especially tools to make tools, and of indefinitely varying their manufacture" and he analogizes it to cinematography, as it consists of segmenting, synthesis and restating (Bergson, 1920, pp. 146, 323); that is, an instance of differentiation and meaning assignment. *Conceptualizing*, much like perception, is an activity that in living systems helps to construct reality, but that in humans helps also to build a notion of the self and the social.

As I stated before, there is a close-knit relationship between perceiving and conceptualizing, where there is constant feedback between both: what we understand is mediated by our sensory input and what I observe and sense is colored by what I comprehend the world to be. As information is the sum of a difference and meaning with the body as a point of reference, the knowledge we generate is not universal and general, but rather is made by a subjective system and is anchored to social and historical context.

Thomas Kuhn's paradigm theory is a great example of this, for he states that knowledge is not linear, but implies a shift of perspectives (Kuhn, 1996). We then conceptualize reality, the self and the social with the ideas we are surrounded with, mediated by perception, but also by language, as will be shown, and we can posit new ideas capable of influence. This, in part, is how culture is disseminated.

Language plays a very important role in human cognitive development: unlike animals that have face-to-face communication that can be comprised of body language, gestures and sounds ("sign games"), humans have a form of communication that not only has a one-to-one basis, but can also be communicated in an abstract way ("language games"). However, language has a particularity that general communication does not: it is self-referential abstraction, whereas things like gestures and body language are concrete self-referential embodied actions. Better phrased, "Language is a special system of communication that can talk about itself" (von Foerster, 1994, p. 116).

Language creates a connection between cognitive systems where the receiver of the information interprets it and relates it with its own experiences and purposes, in order to create knowledge; this is a continuous, dialectic, circular, self-referential process with ever-changing subjects. This is what creates the transition from animal cognition, which has a minimal degree of self-reference, to that of humans, which is fully reflexive. In his research, Piaget summarizes it in the following way: "When the appearance of language intervenes, the child is confronted, not only with a physical universe like before, but with two new worlds ... the social world and the world of internal representations" (Piaget, 1974, p. 32).

The relationship between language and human cognition can be seen more clearly when it is related to the cognitive system in general: Language is set as a cognitive machine that allows the usage of symbols and inner representations; all the other machines, coordinated by A- and P-consciousness, take that input and output and integrate them into a whole that can be restructured as new information comes along.

Taking into account the Sapir-Whorf hypothesis, which states that linguistic patterns determine what the individual perceives in this world and how they think about it, von Bertalanffy states that cognition first depends on the psycho-physical organization of man, while conceptualization is culture-bound because it depends on the symbolic responses that are applied (von Bertalanffy, 1969, pp. 222, 227, 237–238).

This can be represented by means of two dialogical relations, and the first one takes place between language and those that speak it. On the one hand, language is part of the cognitive and cultural backdrop in which a human being develops (that is, "Language produces man"); but on the other hand, human beings in their interaction can change the way language and its components are used (or, "Language is produced by man").

The second relationship is that which takes place between humans and social systems: By interacting with their peers in different ways, humans create social systems, but also human systems, which come to be in the background of social systems. Culture and language are thus "produced" by them. Berger and Luckmann (1967, p. 52) say:

> Social order exists *only* as a product of human activity ... Both in its genesis (social order is the result of past human activity) and its existence in any instant of time (social order exists only and insofar as human activity continues to produce it) it is a human product.

Language allows the creation of culture, which at the same time affects human psychology; culture and the biological aspects of the brain engage in reciprocal causation, a relation as stated by Richerson and Boyd: "... we have an evolved psychology that shapes what we learn and how we think, and that this in turn influences the kind of beliefs and attitudes that spread and persist.... Culture affects the success and survival of individuals and groups.... These culturally evolved environments then affect which genes are favored by natural selection. Over the evolutionary long haul, culture has shaped our innate psychology as much as the other way around" (Richerson, Boyd, 2005, p. 4).

3.3 Cognitive Coherence as the Mediation of Experiential and Logical Cognition

This aspect entails the mediation of logical and experiential cognition; as such, it entails elements of both, using self-reference as a medium. Consciousness in living systems is the interplay of self-computation and phenomenal- and access-consciousness; human cognition builds upon these and adds the coordination of all information to allow subjectivity and story generation from a subjective viewpoint.

This means that human cognition possesses a coordination of information that allows reflexivity, by means of accounting for oneself in an abstract form; this entails language as abstract sign processing and neural mechanisms like mirror neurons and the cortical midline structure. Cognitive coherence entails the mediation of feelings and reason in order to create a coherent narrative of the self, as devoid of contradictions as possible.

Rationality has as a purpose the maintenance of the coherence of the cognitive system, acting as an equilibrator between logical and experiential cognition. There are a myriad of diverging concepts regarding what should count as rationality; for the purpose of this study, rationality will be understood as the human capacity of making sense of things and retaining the coherence of its cognitive domain. While consciousness is the act of binding together differing cognitive threads into a single narrative, rationality is the process of sense-making in which this activity takes place.

Its purpose is to serve as an adaptation mechanism that helps the cognitive domain deal with past and current experience, arranging and rearranging existing information according to a vision of the world, or rearranging that cosmovision in light of inconsistencies – it is, in other words, a coping mechanism. This harmonious process can be summarized from what Piaget describes as adaptation, upon which any cognitive system regardless of its state of development establishes its needs and interests (Piaget, 1974, pp. 17–18):

> Every need tends to: 1st, incorporate the things and people to the activity proper of the subject and, therefore, to "assimilate" the external world to the already built structures, and 2nd, readjust the latter in accordance with the experienced transformations, and therefore, to "accommodate" them to the external objects ... all mental life ... tends to

> assimilate progressively the environment, and makes this incorporation thanks to a set of structures of psychic objects, which ratio of action is ever increasing: Perception and elemental movements first give access to proximate objects on its momentary state, then memory and practical intelligence allow to reconstruct its immediate anterior state and anticipate further transformations. Intuitive thought comes to reinforce both. Logical intelligence, in its form of concrete operations and finally of abstract deduction, ends this evolution by making the subject owner of the most distant happenings, both in space and time.

In the end, *cognitive coherence, as the mediation between experienced and logical cognition*, is the subject of constant accommodation and change, in order to depict a coherent conjunction of both; that is, adaptation and change are within the very essence of human nature. Bergson states it eloquently: "We find that, for a conscious being, to exist is to change, to change is to mature, to mature is to go on creating oneself endlessly" (Bergson, 1920, p. 8).

The cognition of living systems is unified by cognitive coherence, which manifested into identity ("I" and "me") and consciousness. The latter has four distinguishable elements: (1) all internal states are part of the personal consciousness; (2) these states are constantly changing; (3) yet they are perceived as continuous; and (4) they display intention in generating a focus of attention and a resulting periphery (Hudson, 2010, p. 131).

Human beings have their cognitive processes enriched by reflexivity in ways that have already been indicated and this affects the way in which they are unified; unlike animals, they can become self-conscious by means of language as their instrument of objectification (Morin, 2008, p. 78): one has a fully objectified internal dimension, that is, one has a body and experiences having a body. This results in an ongoing loop of objectification and subjectification of the self, which manifests by the interplay of experienced and logical cognition; consciousness is then conceptualized and felt.

Because communication in general gives way to social systems, consciousness also includes the awareness of the other, at the same time that one is aware of himself (von Foerster, 1994, 131). That is, self-reference (and thus consciousness) can be stated both as an irreducible "I" that cannot be accounted for by others, but also as a "we", that can be stated by members of a collective.

One thing of utmost importance is to note that even though others cannot say "I" for me, the way each of us says it varies: von Foerster states that consciousness talks of "how I would like to be but about how I am ..." (von Foerster, 1994, 130); Radin takes the opposite perspective, stating that the mind of a cognizing subject does not necessarily perceive the world as it is, but as they wish it to be (Radin, 1997, p. 254). I think that both perspectives have truth in them for mental models of the world are liable to reflecting expectations, biases and desires in a belief- and ego-friendly manner.

Cognitive coherence in general acts as a "story generator" that creates mental simulations of what is really out there, which are subject to distortion because of the worldview of the cognizing subject (Radin, 1997, p. 254); this means that consciousness is the editor that ensures that the "story" or "model" of reality is as coherent and devoid of contradictions and inconsistencies as possible and in such an endeavor it finds itself in the tension between what it is and what we want it to be.

3.4 How Does This Relate to the Social?

Biologically, the interaction between cognitive machines operates as a parallel distributed neural system that works on several levels; in the nervous system there is a parallel processing in an assembly of neurons that interacts in a way that brings forth the cognitive machine, and a chemical communication between neurons that are not proximate with one another, and serves as communication lines between cognitive machines.

Experiential and logical cognition and cognitive coherence act as a coordination of other mechanisms like perception, memory and concrete sign processing, and at the same time they are coordinated with abstract sign processing in order to yield the information processes that are unified by A- and P-consciousness. This cognitive dynamic is manifested as a heterarchy of cognitive machines: a) Tier 1, memory, perceptual and concrete sign processing; b) Tier 2, experiential and logical cognition, cognitive coherence and abstract sign processing; and c) A- and P- consciousness. They interact as follows:

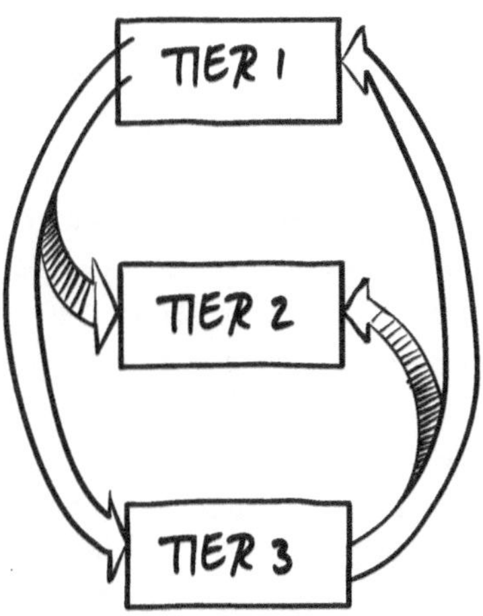

Human cognition, then, has a more abstract and reflexive operation than that of other living systems. However, how does this relate to social interaction? The answer resides in the fact that biology and thermodynamics inform all social behavior; to know the biological facts of social interaction can help to theorize and study it better.

Furthermore, in the practice, political operators have taken advantage of these facts by manipulating collective emotions and perceptions. In *Communication Power*, Castells dedicates a whole section to the relation between emotion cognition and power. He summarizes this idea by stating the relation of power and biology in the following manner: "Power is constructed, as all reality, in the neural networks of our brain. Power is generated in the windmills of the mind" (Castells, 2009, p. 145).

There is a principle in Law that is important to know in these cases: *Ignorantia juris non excusat*, or "ignorance of the law excuses no one"; in this case, to ignore the biological foundations of social behavior does not excuse the fact that we are all subject to them. Interpreted in a negative sense, knowledge of the Law allows one to be excused; this means that if one is aware of the biological foundation of social behavior, one can modify it and manipulate it.

For instance, beliefs affect brain chemistry and thus interfere with cognitive coherence: Differing opinions can trigger a defensive state in humans where neurotransmitters such as norepinephrine interfere with coherent thinking and working memory (the capacity to consciously store and use complex representations to guide goal-directed behavior), causing resistance and interfering with the assimilation of an idea, notwithstanding its usefulness or value. This state is in part provoked and further consolidated by processive or psychogenic stress, which is a type of stress that consists of something being perceived or understood as a threat and thus conferred a stressful quality (Chamberlain, Robbins, 2013).

When views are appreciated, dopamine neurotransmission activates the reward neurons, increasing self-esteem, which is closely linked with serotonin; thus, social validation acts as a reward and increases the levels of dopamine and serotonin. Social relations influence morals and ethics as humans communicate with one another and interact as individuals and groups with the environment (teleology vis-à-vis teleonomy), with actions being a result of the validation obtained or missing from the social structure (Koob, 1992; Chamberlain, Robbins, 2013).

The prefrontal cortex regulates thoughts, actions and emotions by means of extensive interconnection with other brain regions; as this is done repeatedly, logical behavior and emotional resilience are reinforced, and if this is not so, thoughts and actions become impulsive (Arnsten, 2009). Random reaction and lack of conscious choice are unconsciously frustrating, but solved by rationalizing explanations and embedding them into existing memories. Information processing in the human brain is optimal when neural activity is synchronized; when cognitive dissonance takes place, this optimality is compromised and thus there is a drive to reduce dissonance.

All these types of behavior are subject to the maneuvering of political operators, who aim to sway the collective opinion to their cause.

4 *General Sociability*

Social systems function on the basis of cognitive machines, for they are constituted by living systems (both human and animal). Whenever there is sign processing, be it concrete or abstract, there is a point of contact with social systems, for they create a cooperative domain of interactions between subjects through the development of a common frame of reference, although each of them acts exclusively within his cognition (Maturana, Varela 2012, p. 57). Social systems are those where there is such mutual observation (Mancilla, 2011).

Maturana has the theorem "Anything said is said by an observer", which is complemented by von Foerster's "Anything said is said to an observer", and later connected as follows: a) an observer is characterized by being able to make descriptions, b) observers connect through language, c) society is formed by a common usage of language, and d) the interrelation of these concepts is circular: it cannot be determined which one was first (von Foerster). Taking this into consideration it can be said that social systems comprise mutually observing systems, or in better terms: *Anything said is said by an observer to another* (Mancilla, 2011).

Brier takes into account animal social systems, which comprise emotional and instinctual psychological sign games that have their origin in the evolution of species-specific signification processes of living systems and that are manifested in paralinguistic forms; human social systems have linguistic interactions or "language games", products of a social structure, inside of which individual members interact and construct shared realms of meaning. These tiers of social interaction are not mutually exclusive, as human social systems take concrete sign processing (such as facial expressions, hand gestures, and body positions) and sign games as the basis for abstract sign processing and language games.

General sociability is a realm often neglected by those intent on studying human behavior and its intricacies; however, it is very important to do so because all human communication has a non-linguistic component: be it face-to-face where body language, gesticulations, tone of voice and other factors help to transmit information, or impersonal communication, both in the way messages are sent and how they are received.

5 *Human Social Systems*

Language has had a great influence on the development of human cognition, and this holds true for human socialization as well. It has a biological basis in the human brain, where it can be understood to operate as a part of it in charge of processing one or more abstract sign processing systems, and can be defined as a "cognitive system that uniquely allows humans to produce and comprehend meaningful utterances" (Ohio State University, p. 695). On the relationship between human cognition and language, Brier (2008, pp. 399, 401) adds:

> Sign games develop into language games through evolution and through the life experiences of the human impact. As we are born and grow into human social communication, the psyche is perfused with language. As our mind is infected with language, we become linguistic cyborgs – or what we call humans. On this view we are born as animals with the capacity to construct interpenetration between psychic and social-communicative systems, thus creating internal Interpretants that are meaningful to us.

Furthermore, there is an interaction between internal self-observation and mutual observation by means of the interaction of cortical midline structures and the mirror neuron system. Uddin et al. propose a model that accounts for the convergence of self-observation and mutual observation by the complementary interaction of midline structures and mirror neurons: "a right-lateralized mirror neuron system is involved in understanding the multimodal embodied self … whereas cortical midline structures seem to represent a less bodily grounded self as shaped by its social relationships" (Uddin, Iacoboni and Keenan, 2007).

Mirror neurons allow an observer to directly understand the meaning of the actions and emotions of others by internally replicating them without any logical cognition. This helps to bridge first- and third-person perspectives by means of the observation of an action, which leads to its understanding by knowing its outcome (Uddin, Iacoboni and Keenan, 2007). This means that the mirror neuron network allows physical other-to-self mapping, whereas the cortical midline structure underscores the mental state and evaluative simulation. The social validation reward mechanism and the interaction between mirror neurons and the midline structure show the way in which humans are dependent on social validation and driven to fit in, which in turn results in a duality and a tension between self-observation and mutual observation.

Also of importance are *speech acts*, which are "actions that are performed only through using language: a term that describes the use of speech emphasizing the speaker's intention or goal in producing an utterance" (Ohio State University, p. 704). Language as a process and as information resides within the nervous system of autopoietic systems and manifests itself outside of it by means of speech acts. Language and speech acts are necessary for the creation of institutional facts, which are an assignation of function to objects and people by means of a collective intentionality expressed by means of a speech act (Searle, 2010).

The way in which I will explain human sociability will attempt to cut across the well-known categorizations that exist in the disciplines of the social sciences: Law, political science, economics, sociology, anthropology and others. I will do so focusing on three aspects: Viability, Optimality and Adequacy. The first centers on the most basic adaptive behavior that ensures the continued existence of the collectivity, be it big or small; the second comprises the goals that this group gives to itself beyond mere survival; and the third is the mediation of both.

5.1 Viability

Any social system regardless of its scale must have a set of rules and apply them, which I will call *normative order*. First off, it must be said that norms enable legal cognition and communication and can be defined as a project of reality – that is, a hypothetical to which the existing social reality is meant to be molded to. At the same time, because they are manifested in reality, norms form part of reality and thus by their own existence affect social reality (Mancilla, 2015).

A normative order is a system of norms – which can be contradictory – that attempts to mold social reality to its mandates. To this purpose it is constantly applied, which results in its interpretation and sometimes its modification in order to adapt to changes in circumstances. The elements of the normative order are the following: 1) a legal norm, 2) its application, and 3) the resulting interpretation, amendment or informal change that results from it, which in turn feedbacks to the norm and changes it. The normative order is both static and dynamic: it is both a repository of data (legal norms) and the process in which they change (application, interpretation, amendment and informal change) (Mancilla, 2015).

My idea of the legal norm comprises two elements: a) *endonorm*, the core of the norm, which is constituted by legal hypothesis and consequence; and b) *perinorm*, the sociological aspects of the norm that determine its validity and that consist in the conventionalisms and social rules that surround the norms and their application, and also the morals that surround their application and acceptance. As projects of reality, norms can have three different types of content (Mancilla, 2015):

We are before a deontic rule when they norm behavior directly; this is because they state an "Ought to" and are subject to the possibility of violation. They can be expressed by means of this formula: "If A, then ought to be B". An example of it can be: "One commits robbery if …, then the sanction ought to be …" (Kelsen, 1990, pp. xxxii, xxxviii). Technical-conventional rules are those that have to be necessarily observed in order for any action to be considered as legal; they are stated like this: "For A, do B". An example of this type of norm can be found in the issuance of a valid document like a passport: "For obtaining a passport, comply with the following requirements …" (Robles, 1982, p. 41) (Mancilla 2015).

Ontic rules are those that state the existence of elements of the legal system, which are then upheld by the beliefs of all the people that constitute a social system; they can be stated as "X counts as Y in context C" (Searle, 2010, p. 10). An example of this can be seen with money, which exists because of a norm that declares it so and continues to do so because there is a continuous assignation of value to it, and can be stated as "Dollar counts as currency in context of United States of America" (Mancilla, 2015).

Lastly, one can understand the relation that norms have with one another as a chain of circular causal processes where there is mutual influence – in other words, a heterarchy.[8] Van Hoecke describes: "Circularity means that the higher norms within the hierarchy of a legal system not only determine the lower ones, but also in turn, are determined by these" (van Hoecke, 2002, pp. 37–38). This can be expressed as follows (Mancilla, 2015):

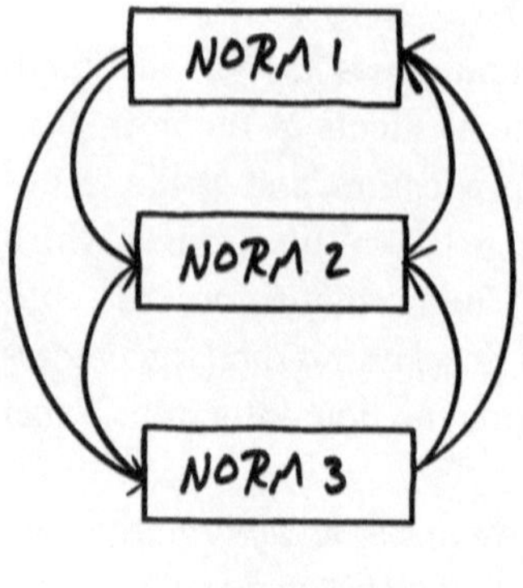

8 This notion was first introduced by Warren S. McCulloch in 1945, in his paper "A heterarchy of values determined by the topology of nervous nets" published in *The Bulletin of Mathematical Biophysics*.

In the case of deontic norms, when a fact fits within the normative hypothesis and the legal consequence is sought, one turns to legal application, which in its most basic form implies a voluntary or a compulsory compliance with the law, with subjects of Law that can be part of a geographically established entity (like the State) and individuals or associations whose existences do not generate geographical demarcations with rules of their own (Mancilla, 2015).

When the norm is applied its scope must be interpreted, and interpretation is a construction of the meaning of the norm; however, when interpretation is insufficient, there can be a mutation or informal change (that is, a change that is outside an amendment procedure), and in this case there is a normative reconstruction that allows the incorporation of new meanings to the norm (Mondugno, 2004, p. 18). All of this can be expressed in the following schema (Mancilla, 2015):

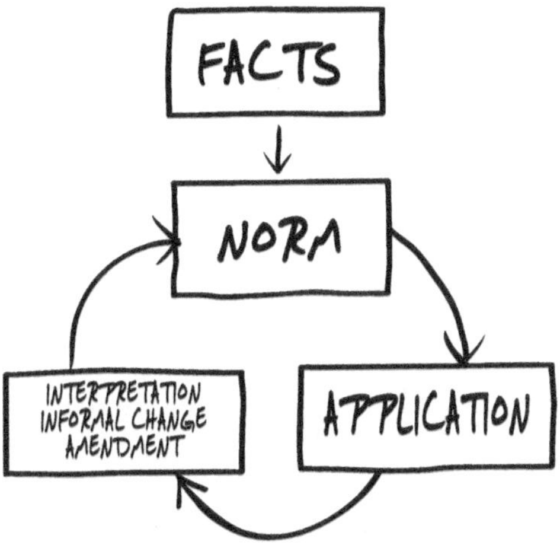

Another important element for this basic model of human sociability is to account for *the satisfaction of material needs at the smallest level possible*, which for the purpose of this analysis will be the household. This resonates with the idea of household economics, which studies the decisions made by members of a residential unit in the quest for welfare (Zeitlin et al.), and with microeconomics, which seeks to understand the behavior of individual producers or consumers in the face of limited resources (Marchant, Snell, 1997).

Despite being applicable to units larger than a household, the model of rules and its application that was posited in prior paragraphs can be of use here, and the same goes for the idea of power and authority that will be advanced. However, it is useful to determine what a household is, and to that Zeitlin et al.

give a definition and then state how it can vary depending on the analysis that is made (Zeitlin et al.):

> Economists focus on the household – a residential unit – whose members pool their resources (at least to some degree) to provide for the welfare of all. Households usually consist of family members linked by blood or marriage, occasionally augmented by unrelated members. Households are defined on the basis of residence, while families are defined primarily by kinship.
>
> The household is not an undifferentiated unit, but "an economy in microcosm, a system of exchanges, entitlements, and responsibilities allocated among members in a group whose boundaries are far from clear" (Rogers 1990). According to Guyer (1980), it is "a particularly dense center in a network of exchange relationships." Within the group residing together, there may be further distinctions between those who do and do not carry out domestic functions together, such as cooking, eating, child care, and farm labour (Webb 1989; Heywood 1990). Therefore different analyses of the same household may identify different subgroups of individuals.

However, this does not mean that there is an intention to understand why a household decides to quell its needs; rather, it seeks to analyze the way in which this takes place, the "how", for it is one of the things that a social system must constantly solve in order to maintain its coherence. That is, the satisfaction of needs studied from the household level as an element of coherence in the social system, without necessarily seeing the effects on a larger scale, is what we are looking for.

For the purpose of this study, we will understand *power* as the capacity to do something. In the context of a social system, which entails mutual observation, power is the capacity of self-organization of the social system towards the pursuit of a perceived goal (Mancilla, 2012). Any social system must have a system that conveys authority and allows one to accede and wield power, and this way, rules can be applied and material needs can be met by the distribution of resources.

Traditional notions of power presuppose a relationship or series of relationships in which one party imposes their will, despite the opposition of others to make them act or abstain; for instance, Loewenstein defines it along the lines of a reciprocal socio-psychological relationship operating between those who hold and exercise power, and those to whom it is directed (Loewenstein, 1965, p. 6).

However, not all acts of power in social relations imply an opposing will. In his article "The Fourth Face of Power", Peter Digeser analyzes several conceptions of power: His first and second faces of power comprise the traditional notion, which he represents by quoting Dahl, Bachrach and Baratz. The third face of power, represented by Steven Lukes, is the manipulation of the desires and the will of a subject, not necessarily the imposition of an action. The fourth face of power, represented by Foucault, consists in the social construction of the individual, and can be understood as the cultural foundation for the other three (Digeser, 1992, pp. 978–979).

The context upon which power is exercised is important: The idea of power in all its configurations takes place in an environment of conflict as it presupposes the access of power, its usage, its maintenance, and the way the spoils are shared among those who band together to reach it. This means that political structures tend to be structured like a game.

This is to be understood as the interaction between two or more players, which has rules that determine the behavior, those who can partake, the strategies available to each player, the sequence in which they can act and the payoffs for each player for all possible combinations of strategies pursued (Zaluski, 2013, p. 24). Wiener states that two examples of social interactions as games are the market and the family game of Monopoly, which simulates it (Wiener, 1961, p. 159).

Because of the game-like nature of political interactions, it is useful to make use of Cyert and March's dominant coalition theory to explain goal-setting in social systems. They view the organization as a coalition of individuals, which can be organized into subcoalitions; the borders of both are never fully set, so they can be redrawn on temporal or functional criteria. The authors depart by stating the problems entailed within a theory of collective goal determination: a) people have goals, but collectivities of people do not; b) collective decision-making requires the implementation of an analogy of individual goals at the individual level (Cyert, March, 2012, p. 31).

They also state the three main procedures by means of which the objectives of a coalition are determined: a) the bargaining process by which the composition and general terms of the coalition are fixed; b) the internal organization process control by which objectives are stabilized and elaborated; c) the process of adjustment to experience by which coalition agreements are altered in response to environmental changes (Cyert, March, 2012, pp. 31, 33).

Another relevant aspect is that of side payments, which can take various forms: money, personal favors, authority, among others; when a winning coalition bargains with itself over side payments, organizational objectives arise and are clarified. However, the agreements on side payments are imperfect, because they cannot foresee all future circumstances: The participants of the bargain have incentives to operate under the framework created by it and to create systems that will enforce it; but also, secondary bargaining regarding these controls can help to specify and elaborate the initial agreement (Cyert, March, 2012, pp. 35, 37–38).

Past experience matters for bargaining in the coalition, as past agreements set precedent for current situations and for future disputes and tensions; the demands of members of the coalition are disorganized and influenced by past situations; these do not receive attention evenly, and they can conflict one with the other with the focus on certain demands being variable. A coalition is viable if the payments to its members are enough to keep them in the group, and when these payments exceed the requirement of cohesion, there is organizational slack (Cyert, March, 2012, pp. 40, 42–43).

The constitution of the coalition is of great importance. However, also important is the cost of their maintenance (as they are open systems) and the effectiveness of the coalition – that is, the cost of power to the power-holder. On this matter Deutsch talks of a concept of net power as "the difference between the amounts of changes accepted by the actor. The changes imposed are those imposed by the actor upon his environment, including changes imposed on relevant antagonists. The changes accepted are those accepted in the values and in the communication and action systems of the actor" (Deutsch, 1966, pp. 114, 116).

5.2 Optimality

In determining what is "ideal" in establishing a goal that goes beyond mere survival, a social system has to determine its *identity, which stems from a shared history and follows through to a sense of destiny*. This is all part of *culture*, which Selznick et al. define as the "shared ways of thinking and believing that grow out of group experience and are passed from one generation to the next" (Selznick, Broom, Broom Darroch, 1981, p. 54).

Richerson and Boyd define it as "information capable of affecting individuals' behavior that they acquire from other members of their species through teaching, imitation and other forms of social transmission", and clarify information as "any kind of mental state, conscious or not, that is acquired or modified by social learning and affects behavior" (Richerson, Boyd, 2005, p. 5).

Humans have a recursive relation with culture: on the one hand, they grow in the context of a cultural and linguistic system that allows them to derive information from existing vehicles, and on the other, they can participate in social systems and become generators of culture.

Culture can be understood as a vehicle when we talk about media by means of which an observer can construct information on what constitutes the content of culture; it can also be a *cosmovision* when it comprises the worldview that one individual can have and which can be shared, mostly or partly with others. Finally, it can also be a process, for it consists of the different cognitive and linguistic processes used by an individual to create information about culture and transmit it, and attempt to create new patterns to be incorporated into existing vehicles.

Social identity is a recursive process on two levels: On the level of individual cognition, it is the programming and reprogramming of the subject that accepts information external to themself as foundations for determining their self-hood. On the level of group information, identity can be constituted by the collective efforts of many individuals. Furthermore, social identity is not homogeneous: It can be constructed at many levels, as one can be a member of a family, a religion, a city, a region or a nation, among many others.

Social identity has many vehicles that convey information that an individual can use for the construction of their identity, like history books, anthems, flags and other media. It also consists in understanding oneself as part of a group and thus part of something larger than oneself, and is a way of understanding oneself within the world. Lastly, it is a dynamic process that is changing within the individual, even if this is not perceived, as one can feel more or less attached to a group over time.

The *distribution of resources on an overall scale past the basic satisfaction of needs* is one of the factors that drive forward the fight for what is the ideal. When there are resources that allow a livable present for a significant number of people, there is room for culture, science and debate. This does not mean the study of macroeconomics, but rather the analysis of the policy and its implementation, that allow for the distribution of resources to satisfy basic needs of a significant sector of the population, and the management of the surplus.

This follows the same logic of the satisfaction of basic needs: the household is still an object of study, for it is a unit of analysis that is useful as it helps to fill in the gap that exists between micro and macroeconomics. However, in this case, the policy impact of the measures taken to guarantee the basic satisfaction and how surplus is (or is not) redistributed is important.

This approach is useful because it traverses approaches to economics, and can be extended to different levels of analysis (for instance, groups of up to twenty persons, communities, cities, states and so on) (Mancilla, 2012), but it can also be used in conjunction with political, legal and sociological approaches, and incorporated into a trans-discipline, like sociocybernetics.

Ideology is information that flows within a social system as possible ideal states of it or directions to take; it has origins within a group, which can be spread through discourse, debate and struggles. Kennedy gives a useful definition: "a universalization project of an ideological intelligentsia that sees itself as acting 'for' a group with interests in conflict with those of other groups ..." (Kennedy, 1997, p. 39).

To him, the intelligentsia is formed by the "people who operate the ideology, who develop it, apply it, and change it sometimes radically, over time ..." (Kennedy, 1997, p. 39); because of this mutability, ideology can be different from the interests that fuel it, but not completely autonomous. Ideology is defined by the tensions that exist between those groups that form the intelligentsia, which results in its permeation through legal materials.

Ideology is enacted into several fora: for one, it drives electoral processes and political debates, and is also within Law when norms that can have ideological content are enacted by a judge who has a certain ideology and policy preferences; it is also within culture, both as content and within the process that creates and spreads it.

Culture as a process starts with the inception of a cultural pattern or the latter's modification; afterwards it is transmitted from a cosmovision to a vehicle, and if it is successful, it results in widespread adoption, although some patterns can fall into obsolescence. This can be visualized as follows:

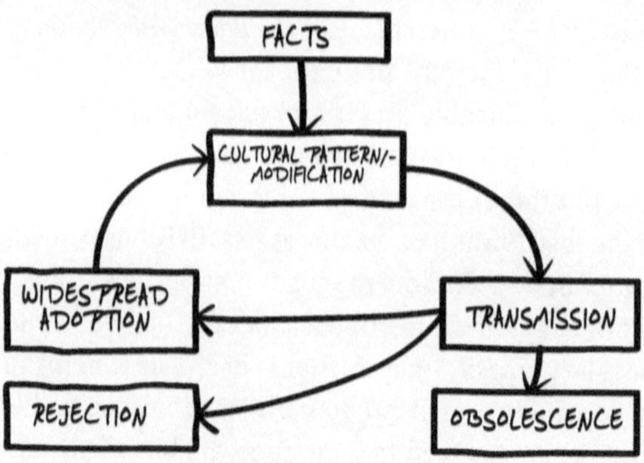

As a process of creation and change, culture can manifest itself in different ways: a) *acculturation*, the adoption of new traits and patterns resulting from interaction with another culture; b) *weakening*, the change in the vehicles that entails a loss of viability within the established framework; c) *renewal*, a change in culture when it is subject to new values, resulting in a restructuration of the existing cosmovision; and d) *destruction*, in which change or external influences sometimes result in the weakening and collapse of the cosmovision (Selznick, Broom, Broom Darroch, 1981, pp. 75–80).

The process of creation and modification of culture and the dynamic and changing nature of human beings guarantee the existence of variation; however, there are also similarities between cultures, referred to by Selznick et al. as cultural universals. Despite the latter, it is not uncommon that each group views their perspective as the natural one, eschewing those different from it; this is known as ethnocentrism and is the manifestation of the ego within culture (Selznick, Broom, Broom Darroch, 1981, pp. 64–65).

5.3 Adequacy

Social systems engage in information processing by means of the activities of their individual constituents. They do so to coordinate and survive, and to determine the overall goals of the system past this basic state. In serving both processes, the social system attempts to construct knowledge. There are diverse forms of obtaining knowledge, which will be called *epistemic projects – knowledge deriving from specialized groups to develop technology and know-how in order to solve problems.*

An epistemic project is a socialized form of constructing a representation of what surrounds a group of cognizing subjects, and is a way in which a social system builds a representation of what surrounds it. They arise in part because social organization requires the invention and implementation of policies to meet new conditions. The creative intelligence function in a society forms an essential aspect of the intellectual resources required for survival and requires attention, manpower and material resources (Deutsch, 1966, pp. 163–164).

When a solution to a problem has been discovered by an individual or group, this must be proposed to others in order to garner acceptance and support in their implementation. Often, new patterns in politics, economics, and culture come from and are transmitted by "social deviants, misfits, strangers, members of minorities and 'marginal men'" (Deutsch, 1966, p. 172). Epistemic projects then comprise a repertoire of information that is considered valid by means of a consensus, in that it has a series of practices that are considered acceptable in constructing knowledge and an authorized group of practitioners.

Science is an epistemic project that takes perceptions of the Universe and offers them to their users to be internalized, debated, and used to generate new observations; that is, they are external-to-internal-to-external. However, it could be argued that Religion and Art are epistemic projects as well – for one, they have a body of knowledge that is accepted by those who partake in them, usually represented in written media as treatises and philosophical positions, a set of rites and procedures for derivation of new knowledge and the reinforcement of the existing one, and a set of authorized practitioners that minister such a cosmovision to those who are interested.

The main difference resides in the fact that Art and Religion rise from internal points of view about the external reality, intending to change the perspective held of it; that is, internal-to-external-to-internal. All epistemic projects have a narrative, or *paradigm* in Kuhn's terms, which is the general explanation of a phenomenon or understanding of things, which can originate from the work of an individual or group in reaction to a problem, which can vary in nature. For example, a philosophical problem may differ from a scientific one, or from an aesthetic one, and different epistemic projects can give different answers to the same problem.

Narratives substitute for one another and can dominate. When this happens, there is a process of elaboration, where practitioners work to justify it and solve problems that arise from the adaptation of reality to the narrative; periods of crisis, where the narrative cannot accommodate emerging problems; and a period of narration substitution, where there is a shift (Kuhn, 1996, p. 36).

This is of course based on Kuhn's approach to scientific revolutions, but one can see that even in Art, Religion, Philosophy, and beyond, where there is no need for proof and experiments, there are changes in narrative that usually take place every generation in the form of a sudden shift, rather than a set of cumulative changes.

Narratives are the point of origin of the activities of an epistemic project, as they give way to their rules, practices, specialized usages of language and equipment, applications, and professionalization processes which acculturate soon-to-be practitioners into viewing the world in a determinate way. Narratives can be composed of other specialized narratives, which can dominate and shift into others with different pacings; thus, Kuhn stated that there could be both big and small scientific revolutions (Kuhn, 1996, pp. 42, 46, 49).

In justifying their existence, epistemic projects tend to create a linear historical narrative of progress, upon which all the different paradigmatic narratives and resulting shifts that have comprised it are unified into one picture, which can be stated in the form of different materials for the purpose of informing others (Kuhn, 1996, p. 36).

A narrative entails, within a practitioner, a way of understanding what surrounds him, a commitment to such a worldview and an implicit rejection of competing formulations that can imperil its dominance. Thus, there is a risk of emotional attachment on the part of the practitioner when there is an investment of time and effort to the dominance of their narrative; that is, narratives are ego-based and sometimes make debate difficult. Despite the possibility of sharing it with others, the worldview is relative to the beholder, and shifts in narrative are revolutionary only to those whose worldview is affected; outsiders view it as part of the developmental process (Kuhn, 1996, pp. 84, 85).

Furthermore, shifts from one narrative to another entail a process of partial destruction and reconstruction of the epistemic project as an institution, as its fundamentals are affected, as well as existing methods and applications. Shifts in narrative also imply a change in the activities of practitioners, both in their methods, instruments, problems to address and their possible solutions, as well as in the goals of the institution (Kuhn, 1996, pp. 93, 109).

In epistemic projects that have experimental and verification activities, a narrative and its possible change influences the way in which information and data are derived and interpreted. As has been shown, this is because knowledge is constructed by a cognitive system, and thus it is not a given; because a narrative is internal to the observer, the latter has to be mindful in the way it observes, as it can affect the outcome of the experiment. Furthermore, relevant results are influenced by the narrative and different worldviews entail varying forms of research (Kuhn, 1996, pp. 122, 126).

In mediating a set of ideals and survival by means of social organization, *social systems often allow individuals or groups to perform certain actions or commit to providing a service, or prevent something from happening.* This is exemplified in the West with the idea of human rights, which are defined by Osiatyński as "… universal moral rights of fundamental character. They belong to every person in his or her relations with the state and with any other authority in a position to use coercive power against the individual … human rights are inherent and belong to the human being *as such.* It is believed that every person comes to existence endowed with these rights" (Osiatyński, 2009, p. 23).

However, human rights are much more complex than this definition, with several theories and conceptions of human rights with their own histories, and rising to address different concerns and needs; this happens because of the importance that they bear in areas such as international relations, politics, Law, and so on (Twining, 2009, pp. 173–174).

The notion of individual rights matured during the Enlightenment, where the idea of the rights of man came to be and with it the notion of a limited government (Tamanaha, 2004, p. 26). One can signal the following individual rights: right to life (art. 6 International Covenant on Civil and Political Rights, hereafter ICCPR), prohibition of torture (7 ICCPR), prohibition of slavery (8 ICCPR), rights to liberty and security of person (9–10 ICCPR), freedom of movement (12 ICCPR), right to privacy (17 ICCPR), freedom of thought (18 ICCPR), freedom of religion (18 ICCPR), freedom of expression (19 ICCPR), and freedom of association (21 and 22 ICCPR). They are an (ideally) enforceable prerogative that the governed possess against the government and its usage of authority, which is used to guarantee certain valued goods: life, security, thought, expression, and religion, among others.

Dignity is the fundamental principle of human rights. It can be found in the most important human rights treaties and can be defined as "a distinctive feature of human beings regarding the rest of living beings, which constitutes the human person as an end by itself, preventing it from being considered as an instrument or as means to other ends. Such dignity constitutes itself as the source of all human rights" (Nogueira Alcalá, 2007). This idea not only entails the justification of individual rights, but also gives way to the inclusion and implementation of Social Welfare Rights, which are known as "second-generation" rights.

The Universal Declaration of Human Rights lists the following rights: Access to social security and social, cultural and economic rights (Article 22), Right to Work and Protection Against Unemployment (Art. 23.1), Right to Just and Fair Conditions of Employment (Art. 23.2), Right to Form Trade Unions (Art. 23.4), Right to Rest and Leisure (Art. 24), Right to an Adequate Standard of Living for the Health and Well-Being of Himself and of His Family (Art. 25.1.), Right to Education (Art. 26), and the Right to Participate in Social and Cultural Life (Art. 27.1). The International Covenant of Economic, Social and Cultural Rights elaborates on some of the aforementioned rights, as is the case of the Right to Adequate Food (Art. 11 ICESR), Right to Adequate Housing (Art. 11 ICESR), Right to Education (Art. 13 and 14 ICESR), and Right to Health (Art. 12 ICESR), which are based on the Right to an Adequate Standard of Living (Art. 25.1 UDHR).

In their book *Law and Society in Transition: Toward Responsive Law*, Nonet and Selznick create a typology of legal systems or orders by which one can measure existing ones: repressive, autonomous and responsive law. The authors argue that more than types of Law, these models represent stages of evolution of the relationship between Law and the political and social order; thus, the transition towards progressive forms of Law is the result of *mobilization of interests and negotiations* (Nonet, Selznick, 1978, p. 18).

The main features of their third aspect, responsive law, consist of the opening of legal participation, the role of Law and the instrumentation of social ordering and change through legal institutions. However, too much openness will hamper the ability of legal institutions to moderate the role of power in society, and with this there is the risk of regression – responsive systems then have at their core a tension between openness and fidelity to the law. Responsive systems seek a balance in addressing their core tension by means of pursuing ways in which both openness and integrity sustain each other (Nonet, Selznick, 1978, pp. 74, 76–77).

Responsive systems perceive social pressures as sources of knowledge and opportunities for self-correction, and to do so, they must set an objective purpose, but which is also sufficiently adaptive to control and rule-making. Responsive law thus searches for "implicit values in rules and policies". Instead of seeking only the implementation of an order and a logical structure, the existence of purpose brings the implementation of values in an attempt to find balance (Nonet, Selznick, 1978, pp. 77, 79, 82–83).

Regarding the application of rules, there is a balancing of values and moral and practical reasoning permeate in legal variety. Legal participation increases in volume and intensity. The system transforms the legal forum into a political arena, which can be exemplified by the rise of social advocacy, where the appeal to legal authority and rules is carried with the idea of furthering the interests of a group and the hope of changing legal rules (Nonet, Selznick, 1978, pp. 89, 97).

As I have said before, constitutional theory was built from theoretical frameworks that stem from the Enlightenment, which also includes the obtention of knowledge, or *epistemology*. Social science deals with living beings and thus, it is inseparable from their biology: lawyers, political scientists and others have cared little to connect social theories with cognitive science and philosophy of the mind (let alone cybernetics).

The *3 by 3 by 3 model* attempts to make a framework that traverses different branches of the social sciences, which at times do not communicate as they have differing methods, interests and objects of study; it also purports to create a bridge that can communicate cognitive and social sciences in order to create a simple but thorough overview of human social interaction, which can be adapted to different levels of analysis. All of this will give us the tools we need to recast political theory and constitutionalism into a shape that better fits the times we live in. It is not a total and self-contained development, but can be the stepping stone for more ambitious attempts.

Conclusions to Section 1

The first part is meant to show that the best understanding of phenomena are those based on transdisciplinary approaches; that is, there must be concepts that transcend the different ways of carrying out scientific endeavors. Circular causality is common in the computer sciences as well as biology, and as was shown, also in social phenomena.

Social endeavor also accounts for adapting to an environment, both on an individual level and as a group, and what counts as such varies with the context. Social systems are networks of agents and institutions acting under certain rules, which are made and remade with the passage of time. The complexity of social phenomena might have different measures that vary from one context to another, both in the possibility of being used and of being the ideal tool.

To understand the social is to understand that it is comprised by living beings that breathe, move, eat and have needs that require satiation after a certain period of time. Social systems are dynamic, and thus the frameworks that we conceive to explain them must account for this.

The lack of accounting of this quality by the state, constitution, separation of powers and public/private distinction will be one of the most consistent critiques made, and the main features of what we will offer as an alternative: a living, breathing, moving constitutionalism.

SECTION 2

Introduction

Once we have stated the basic notions of cybernetics that will be used, as well as a model of human social behavior that will serve as the foundation for this part, we will be in the position of engaging in the 'recasting'. As I have said in the introduction, this is a two-part process: first, *a critical dismantling of the basic elements of constitutionalism with the creation of a generic theoretical model and its critique*, and second, *the offering of an alternative based on cybernetics that solves the problems that plague the first model.*

Yes, this in part is a strawman argument, for I do not state the position of a specific author; but these are constructions of the Western understanding of politics, and thus, it is a tradition, transmitted from one generation to the other, thought of as a bedrock or a foundation.

The elements of constitutionalism that I will take into account are those that are listed by the *Stanford Encyclopedia of Philosophy* (Preuss, 2012, p. 23; Stanford Encyclopedia of Philosophy, Constitutionalism): a) statehood, b) sovereignty, c) separation of powers, d) public/private distinction, and e) international/national distinction.

Elements a), b) and d) coalesce into two generic models that I will critique: *state and constitution*. I will also address *separation of powers and the public/private distinction*. Then I will proceed to the sum of them, manifested as a constitutionalism based on cybernetics and made for current times.

Part 3: Recasting the State

1 *Theory of the State*

1.1 A Generic Model

Etymologically, the word "state" comes from the Latin *status*, of "stare" and "be", and was used to refer to a "state of coexistence at a certain moment with the ordering of coexistence". From the 15th century, this term was used in several ways until Machiavelli – according to Jellinek – introduced it into political literature (Serra Rojas, 1964, p. 159).

The *state* can be defined as the political organization of a group of people in a determinate territory. Some authors add to this notion: Burdeau sees it as the repository of political power in which it is institutionalized (Burdeau, 1992, pp. 24, 29–31) while Aurelio García speaks of the existence of a legal organization (Borja, 1991, p. 25). Taking into account these aspects, a minimum concept of the state is the organization of a social group within a territory, with a purpose of permanence, looking to serve a goal that is constantly renewed.

A state has a *territory* when there is a geographical space where the population organizes and develops, which can be understood in different contexts: it is the base of the population, the spatial scope for the exercise of state power, and the field for application of politics. The *government* is the group of individuals empowered by the population to make the decision that will determine its course; this concept is legal and political, because the authority is appointed by procedures contained in legal norms and it looks towards its application. The *population*, says Naranjo Mesa, is "a conglomerate socially, politically and legally constituted" (Naranjo Mesa, 2006, pp. 99, 116); that is, a population is a set of individuals established within a territory, politically organized, with a degree of cohesion, recognized by a normative order and organized by it.

Lastly, there is an additional element to consider: *sovereignty*. To Serra Rojas it is not an unlimited power; rather, it is a feature of its power that consists in enforcing itself internally in its territory, and externally vis-à-vis other states (Serra Rojas, 1964, pp. 342–343). There have been authors that have discussed at length if sovereignty is an element of the state or a mere complement, for there are vassal states, which might be considered as mere annexes of another, or those that have subsumed their sovereignty to another. This is not relevant to the model we are trying to build, but it does help to show one of the most problematic features of state theory.

Two relevant concepts in the theory of the state are the *forms of state and government*. The first can be defined as the way that the elements of the state are organized overall, and the second as the form in which the organs of government form a structure. Borja distinguishes between state and government: "The word State designates the totality of the polity, that is, the set of people – governors and governed – and institutions that form the legally organized society in a determinate territory; on the other hand, the word government comprises only the specific organization of the power constituted in the service of the State" (Borja, 1991, p. 82).

Regarding the *forms of government*, Borja classifies them into *monarchy and republic*. Camacho takes a more historical approach, where he divides them further, into that which is prior to constitutionalism (monarchy, oligarchy and democracy) and posterior to it (monarchy and republic) (Borja, 1991, p. 82). The form of government is a conductive structure of the *who*, that is materialized in the moment where certain members of the population get together to create organs by which the collective intention will manifest itself to bring about the usage of capacity.

The *forms of state are two: simple and composite*. Naranjo says that the first takes place when "there exists only a center of political and administrative drive, that is, in which sovereignty is exercised directly on all the social conglomerates established in the same territory". In the other, "sovereignty is not exercised in a uniform and constant manner in all national territory, but its exercise is fractioned between diverse entities, put in a similar legal and political situation within the state, and that enjoy of an autonomy almost absolute for the management of their own affairs and for the exercise of certain functions" (Naranjo Mesa, 2006, pp. 305, 309).

Taking the last paragraph into account, the forms of state are divided into centralization (simple) and federalism (composite) and are the way in which the usage of power within a certain territory is exercised, regardless of the structure of government that is being incorporated.

In the forms of state, the capacity is conducted by means of *how*, so once the structure of government is set, the way in which it will manifest in the state's territory must be clarified. In a simple form of the state, capacity is exercised by means of the chosen modality of government, having delegations in strategic parts of the territory of the state, but with a coordinating center in which policy is decided. An example of this can be found in France, which although is decentralized to a degree, is divided into administrative departments.

In the complex form of the state exists many points of policy decision and policy-making, which are autonomous from the center and possess their own structure of *who*, and by which they use capacity, separate from the national government which acts within a parallel plane having its own competence. An example of this is the federal system that is implemented in many countries, among them the United States.

To illustrate thoroughly the difference between forms of state and government, it is useful to give some examples. The United States has a composite form of state, for it is a federal system, and unlike monarchic states, it has a republican form of government, which is manifested in a presidential system. France has a simple form of state, for it is centralized, and its form of government is a semi-presidential republic.

1.2 Critique

The first thing to note about *the state as a framework*, is that it is *static and reductive*. This is in part an unfair criticism, as this theory was created well before cybernetics, systems and complexity, but it falls short in current times and we need to assess why. In the first place, it is a model that presupposes that the object of study is merely a sum of its parts, without taking into account that the latter can amount to more. For instance, there are the implications of segments of the population of a state that are mobile, like tribes, or phenomena like internal migration (Kuhn, 2015); the presence of a government in another state, as with embassies and consulates;[9] and the personnel of the latter, who are governmental officials and in general, migrants, who can vote in their country of origin.[10]

On the other hand, *it does not take fully into account how the state interacts with its environment*, which is to some degree unfair to note, as it goes against its simplicity, which is in part what has made it endure through to these times. This for instance is the case of how a state interacts with transnational corporations, which at times can hold more power and influence than some states; however, the idea of sovereignty handles state to state relations. Also, the state as part of a globe in terms of geography and climate is not addressed.[11]

Sovereignty is understood as a binary state, where either there is an assertion of the state's power and authority within its own borders or there is not, and where it is completely independent from foreign powers or it is subjugated. This completely ignores international politics, where there are many nuances in the use of sovereignty, as is the case of submission to the jurisdiction of an international tribunal[12] or when a country uses economic power to exert

---

9 My home country, Mexico, is the country with the most robust consular network in the world. See: Secretaría de Relaciones Exteriores, (2016) *Mexico has the world's largest consular network*, available at: https://www.gob.mx/sre/articulos/mexico-has-the-world-s-largest-consular-network (Accessed: 20 January 2020).

10 This is also the case of Mexico. See: Instituto Nacional Electoral, *Voto de los mexicanos residentes en el extranjero*, available at: http://www.votoextranjero.mx/web/vmre/como-votar (Accessed: 20 January 2020).

11 For instance, we have the Paris Agreements, available at: https://unfccc.int/process-and-meetings/the-paris-agreement/the-paris-agreement.

12 For instance, the Inter American Court of Human Rights: http://www.corteidh.or.cr/historia-en.cfm.

influence.[13] Also, the nuances of national security are bypassed, for we ignore regions in the world that are governed partially or completely by criminal organizations or paramilitary groups.

As populations are recognized by governments, *multicultural groups that are within the state are often ignored in the name of national unity or cohesion*; this is the case of Afro-Mexicans, who despite existing for hundreds of years have only recently been recognized in the Mexican Constitution as a protected class (El Universal). Often there is confusion between population and nation, where the former is a socio-political concept and the latter is merely sociological.

Also, national groups that are dispersed among the borders of two or more states are ignored or taken as an externality, in order to keep things simple. For instance, we have the Roma people in Europe, or the Irish Travellers, who are dispersed and move between Ireland, Canada, the United States and Great Britain.

2 *The Viable System Model*

A frame that can encompass the organization of social systems in general is that of the *Viable System Model*, brought forth in the classic book *The Brain of the Firm*. Beer applied this model to the Chilean nationalized economy while working as a consultant for President Salvador Allende, in what became known as Project Cybersyn or Synco (Beer, 2012). This framework is made as an analogy of the human brain, emphasizing the distinction between the system and its environment and the survival of the former in the latter; the aspect pertaining to viability then consists in a system maintaining its identity separate from its surroundings.

2.1 Original Model

The Viable System Model makes use of homeostasis as a desired state, and to achieve it, a system must deal with internal and external variety, thus amplifying its own variety or attenuating that of its environment in order to obtain similar levels. However, to do so it must act recursively, as it presupposes itself within its model of the environment; this is expressed in the Good Regulator Theorem made by Roger Conant and Ross Ashby, which states that under very broad conditions, the simplest and most effective approach for a controller is to be isomorphic with the controlled, that is (Conant, Ashby, 1970, pp. 89–97), the best solution to a problem must be a representation of it.

13 For instance, China and the economic corridor dubbed the 'Silk Road': https://www.weforum.org/agenda/2017/06/china-new-silk-road-explainer/.

Scholten paraphrases this in very simple terms: Every good regulator of a system must be a model of that system; every good key must be a model of the lock it opens; control implies resemblance, and identical situations imply identical responses (Scholten). This also means that to solve a problem, one has to visualize it as completely as possible, for one cannot enact an effective model of the problem with incomplete information.

Now, the Viable System Model is comprised of five systems and the interactions that they make into two subsystems. *System 1* is in charge of the fundamental operations within the viable system, those that justify the existence of the system, but do not comprise the functions of senior management or officials; this is known as implementation. The internal functioning of this system equals the total internal functioning of the whole system: System 1 is always a viable system by itself, and is its own beginning and end (Livas, 1988, pp. 159–160).

When System 1 overcorrects itself in its attempt to reach a dynamic state, it incurs in oscillation; *System 2* is in charge of balancing one or several Systems 1, and there can be a plurality of Systems 2 due to different oscillatory sources. The function of System 3 is to handle the day-to-day activities of the viable system, which include the supervision of the anti-oscillatory functions of System 2. It is also responsible for replenishing necessary variety when the latter has been filtered out by the managerial activities of the lower systems, which is done by audits, work studies and taskforce activities (Beer, 2012, pp. 74, 82, 86).

System 3 can be of two types: *System 3*, which is in charge of the directing functions of the day-to-day, and *System 3**, which is in charge of replenishing the existing variety by auditing. *The internal processes of the Viable System are dealt by the communication between Systems 3–2-1*, the activities of which have been dubbed by Beer as "*the inside and now of the organism*" (Beer, 2012, p. 107).

System 4 is in charge of the long-term planning and development functions of the viable system. Because of the recursive nature of the VSM, to operate System 4 requires the creation of a model of itself and also enough freedom to learn, adapt and evolve by means of the simulation of reality (Livas, 1988, p. 166). This system also provides self-awareness for the System in focus (Beer, 2012, p. 115). System 5 controls the identity of the viable system and is in charge of defining its objectives; it intervenes between the activities of Systems 3 and 4, which might not share the same priorities, and helps to conciliate them (Livas, 1988, p. 169).

Together, *Systems 3, 4 and 5 constitute the "outside and then" function of the Viable System*, because they are in charge of handling the interaction of the system with the environment. That is, these systems form a metasystem which is "over and beyond" systems of lower logical order (Beer, 2012, pp. 115, 134). Overall, a Viable System Model can be expressed in the following way:

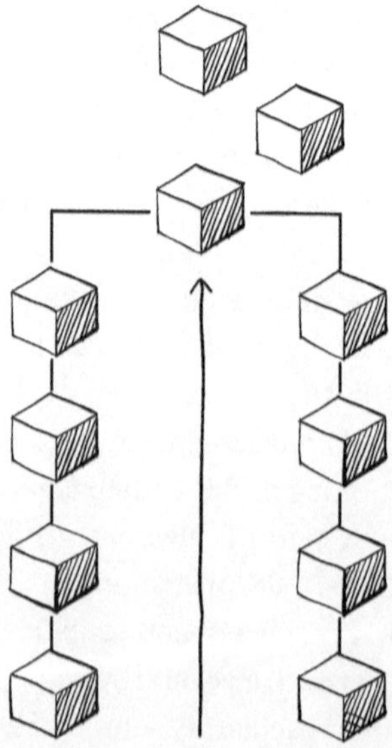

2.2 Modified Viable System Model

The original model was a product of its time, and despite aging quite well, it does not take the observer into consideration in a consistent way, and it does not establish a way to address complexity. Thus, a modified version of the VSM will be offered to the reader in this section, in part by taking into account what Raul Espejo and Alfonso Reyes state in their book *Organizational Systems: Managing Complexity with the Viable System Model*, as their main contribution consists of the incorporation of second-order cybernetics.

In explaining the importance of the observer and thus giving an epistemology of organizations, Espejo gives a useful account of the nature of the VSM:

> Here we offer the Viable System Model (VSM) as problem solving heuristic ... It is built using the concept of variety, a measuring of complexity, which helps to map the proliferating states of our day-to-day situations.

Espejo and Reyes tell us that *systems are mental constructions of those that observe reality* and that *they serve as epistemological devices that help describe something or explore situations* – "We experience and talk about systems, but we do not bump into systems 'out there'. We name them and by doing this we are bringing them into existence". Systems are then the product of an arbitrary distinction that possesses three parts ("the 'inside', the 'outside' and the 'border'"), with a purpose ascribed to it and that has as a frame of reference the subject that makes them. Naming that distinction and meaning consolidates the whole cognitive process (Reyes, Espejo, 2011, p. 4).

This cognitive process is made and bound by a biological structure that is shared by all human beings and that shapes all the interactions that we as such have; environment and sociocultural context are also factors of influence in the way distinctions are made. The world we live in is one of constant interactions that lead to common perceptions, and we help mold and are shaped in turn by them (Reyes, Espejo, 2011, p. 6).

To define a system, then, a group of individuals needs to create a concept (distinction and meaning) that is self-contained: it has clear components and relations and lies within a specific sociohistorical context. However, distinction and meaning can be (re)negotiated among those that partake in them and are a form of social interaction.

Naming and defining, as well as the identity of the stakeholders of the system (and its definition) are the centerpiece of Espejo and Reyes' organizational scholarship, which is a second-order cybernetics approach. In interacting with systems (or our representations of them), there are two approaches that can be taken: 1) to see the system from its environment by distinguishing it from other things and ascribing properties to it, which include inputs, outputs and environmental constraints; and 2) to see the system from within, where the properties of the system are observed from the interaction of its component parts and the environment; there are no inputs or outputs (Reyes, Espejo, 2011, pp. 9–10).

Communication in human social systems entails recurrent interactions within an existing sociocultural context and a joint history; said interactions are constituted by language and emotions, which in turn lead to emergence. That is, the languaging and emotions that constitute communications lead to meanings that go beyond individual conversations or interactions (Reyes, Espejo, 2011, p. 30). Emergence is the domain of complexity, and the latter is a concept which is created by human beings within a social context (Reyes, Espejo, 2011, p. 33).

This leads us to a second-order definition of complexity, for it is not an intrinsic property of a situation, but rather is "an attribute ascribed by observers according to the number of distinctions that they are able to make in the domain in which they interact with that particular situation" (Reyes, Espejo, 2011, pp. 33–34).

It is very important to note that perceived complexity is also dependent on the means used to interact with it; thus, the metrics for complexity are context-dependent. Although variety can be a measure of complexity, it is the subject that determines what the set of possibilities are. Ashby gives us a good example of this (Ashby, 1965, 123, 124):

> ... the act of "communication" necessarily implies the existence of a *set* of possibilities, i.e. more than one, as the following example will show.

> A prisoner is to be visited by his wife, who is not to be allowed to send him any message however simple. It is understood that they may have agreed, before his capture, on some simple code. At her visit, she asks to be allowed to send him a cup of coffee; assuming the beverage is not forbidden, how is the warder to ensure that no coded message is transmitted by it? He knows that she is anxious to let her husband know whether or not a confederate has yet been caught.
>
> The warder will cogitate with reasonings that will go somewhat as follows: "She might have arranged to let him know by whether the coffee goes in sweetened or not – I can stop that simply by adding lots of sugar and then telling him I have done so. She might have arranged to let him know by whether or not she sends a spoon – I can stop that by taking away any spoon and then telling him that Regulations forbid a spoon anyway. She might do it by sending tea rather than coffee – no, that's stopped because, as they know, the canteen will only supply coffee at this time of day." So his cogitations go on; what is note-worthy is that at each possibility he intuitively attempts to stop the communication by enforcing a reduction of the possibilities to one – always sweetened, never a spoon, coffee only, and so on. As soon as the possibilities shrink to one, so soon is communication blocked, and the beverage robbed of its power of transmitting information. The transmission (and storage) of information is thus essentially related to the existence of a *set* of possibilities ...
>
> Communication thus necessarily demands a set of messages. Not only this is so, but the information carried by a particular message depends on the set it comes from. *The information conveyed is not an intrinsic property of the individual message ...*

A Viable System is in communication with its ambiance and thus, the information that it derives from it stem from the possibilities that it has before itself. *Variety is in the eye of the observer.* Espejo and Reyes understand that when they say that "... the distinctions we *actually* make are the *complexity* of the system; its *variety*, on the other hand, is defined by all the *possible* states that we can compute" (Reyes, Espejo, 2011, pp. 33, 35–36).

Any Viable System Model must be the tension of three things: 1) what they are able to perceive; 2) what they can conceive or cognize; and 3) their range of action. This leads to the fact that not only complexity, but also what counts as variety lies within the beholder; as a result, there may be different accounts of variety in the systems of the VSM. And because social systems do not have a collective mind, items 1) and 2) can be points of negotiation and contention to those that vie to lead the VSM. This means that the visualization of the field, so to speak, is a point where resources will be expended; this is also the case with item 3), for the action of the VSM upon perceived and conceived variety is a subject of struggle, as it does not happen for itself. In short: politics is present in all social systems.

The nature of the observer vis-à-vis its capacity for action also changes how we understand variety: there can be perceived variety as well as conceived variety, and they are in constant feedback. New ways of thinking (and thus conceiving) amplify the capacity to perceive variety; conversely, our capacity of thinking variety is yoked by our capacity to perceive it.

As the perception of variety is changing, so does what counts as a state that allows the system to remain adaptive. There is then an element of uncertainty, as current choices determine future problems and one can never have a complete measurement of what surrounds the social system.

In Beer's original design, the VSM aimed towards a homeostatic state by means of the matching variety; however, homeostasis is a state of unchanging equilibrium to which a system returns if there is a perturbation. In Beer's VSM, homeostasis is more of a changing state, even if this difference is not elaborated; this means that Beer intended the VSM to be self-organizing, not homeostatic in the strict sense.

The Viable System Model must study not what a system actually does vis-à-vis what it intends to do, but the tension between these two behaviors; that is, between survival and goal-setting, for all social systems are in a constant tension between teleology and teleonomy, and the transition between homeostasis and dynamic equilibrium.

Self-organization and the social processes that this entail are subject to politics – this means that the stakeholders (who can be inside or outside the system) in the identity of an organization are subject to this, as different conceptions of group identity benefit some groups more than others. There must be in each system a mapping of who the stakeholders are, in and out of the system.

Lastly, because the VSM has an inherent tension between what the organization does to adapt vis-à-vis what it thinks is its ideal state, dominant coalition theory as described in the first part of this study could be used to understand the dynamic of Systems 1–5 and the 1–2–3 and 3–4–5 configurations.

3 *The State as a Viable System Model*

Taking into account both the idea of the state and a modified version of the Viable System Model, we have the elements to recast the state in the light of a sociocybernetics approach. The first thing to understand is that *the state is a convergent reality*: the sum of different perceptions of reality that emanate from the social organization.

In consideration of the *3 by 3 by 3 model*, the state as a convergent reality comprises perceptions about the organization of human behavior in a social context (*legal*); the decisions about the direction of the community (*political*); the use of natural resources possessed by the collectivity (*economical*); the interaction between the different social groups within the population that forms the state (*sociological*); and cohesive cultural elements in which there is a common history and a sense of collective destiny (*historical*).

The goals of the state can be defined and redefined by its populations and they are not activities that can be exhausted: as there are new generations that take the place of those prior to them, each has its own objectives besides the common good, and thus, its finality is constantly renewed. However, it must be examined that if there were no population, the state would cease, so it is considered that the goals of the state can only conclude when it is no more.

The three elements of the state – population, territory and government – coalesce into several Viable System Models: First, the borders of the state help to determine its boundaries (system vs. environment), which can be other states. Second, its population supplies the components by which the organizational aspect of the model is made, but also, forms a network of relations that help determine what it does. Finally, the government is in part the operational component of the state and sovereignty constitutes the way in which the system establishes and resets its boundaries.

A state is a VSM, but is also the environment of others and can even be part of a larger system[14] (Livas, 1988, 159, 160). The first aspect takes place if one sees it vis-à-vis with others, be it in individual relations or as a member of an international community; secondly, there can be smaller governments like cities or states that operate in the state territory and that interact with a national or federal government; thirdly, a state can be a member of an international organization like the OAS or the UN or even a regional government, as is the case of the European Union, all of which can be studied as VSMs of different ilk. A useful heuristic is to imagine these relationships as a set of Russian dolls, which also implies several levels of self-reference:

14 This observation was made originally by Beer in *Brain of the Firm*, but Livas first applied it to the state.

However, this does not mean that the nongovernmental is not contemplated: ethnic, religious and political groups can be seen with a sociocybernetic lens as a VSM that operates within a state or across its borders; this is also the case with nongovernmental organizations and many other groups which can additionally encompass criminal associations. One person can belong to many of these associations (even the government) and they can set their environment (which includes the state) and operate on a perception of internal and external variety, going from homeostasis to dynamic equilibrium and even hypercomplexity. This complex social interaction is described in a concrete way by Major Robert K. Calhoun and Captain Brendan F. Hayward of the Australian Army (Calhoun, Hayward, 2007):

> Complex adaptive systems consist of agents which comprise all the component actors of the system or society. These agents may be individuals, groups or systems. They include governments, political parties, local leaderships, potential or actual insurgents and their supporters, security forces, businesses, religious groups, gangs, criminal elements, schools, universities, the media and non-government organisations. The agents interact with one another and their environment continuously in both deliberate and spontaneous ways. Some of the consequences of these interactions are linear and predictable; others are not ...

I propose the following configuration of the Viable System Model, when we see the state is regarded in relation to others:

- *System 1*: The population of the state is what constitutes the implementation aspect of the VSM and thus it comprises this system.
- *System 2*: Local governments are those that address the immediate oscillations of the population, as they are the closest to the people.
- *System 3*: Regional units of national governments or state governments are those in charge of handling the day-to-day activities of a system; this

includes the separation of powers (Executive, Legislative and Judiciary). Specialized governmental units can act as a System 3*.

- *System 4*: The executive branch of government, as well as the heads of the legislative and judiciary and other high-level organs are those in charge of planning.
- *System 5*: Social mobilizations, political groups and parties and groups that act as intelligentsias are those that struggle to determine the identity of the state.

Each of these systems has a dominant coalition that determines its fate: In System 1, community leaders or other relevant actors can act as such on a small scale which can be broadly replicated; in a System 2, there is a major and its council ruling with the help of political allies; in a System 3 we have regional delegates, legislators (both federal/national and local), judges (same) and others. System 4 has the head of government and/or state and its cabinet, a Supreme Court acting in full chambers and political majorities in a Legislative Assembly. However, in the conjunction of Systems 1–2-3 and 3–4-5 there are also dominant coalitions.

It is important to stress the role that perception plays in a state as a VSM: First, there is a perception of internal and external variety in each of the systems that comprise it, with dominant coalitions determining such roles; second, the state as a whole has such a perception, as do those that act within it. That is, the capacities and problems of the state are perceived by those within and beyond its boundaries, and concrete action by the state is mediated by this.

Let us put forth a very recent example: As I wrote this, the COVID pandemic was raging across the world and I wrote a dossier analyzing it from a complex systems perspective. The factors that make this illness complex are the explosive growth of contagion (external variety) *vis-à-vis* the response capacity of states (internal variety). All this translates into a curve that may or may not cross a line, which represents the capacity of medical systems.

There is an uncertainty in the detection of cases and thus, confirmed cases are not a total detection of the number of people infected in a country; that is, the curve might be bigger than what we track. Conversely, the capacity of health systems might not be as high as we assume, for there could be understaffed hospitals, lack of equipment and other problems that were not registered in official accounts. And between both, there are social distance and isolation measures imposed by the state.

All of this comprises the state as a social system that can define and redefine its boundaries, acting on the perceived variety of an environment and a notion of its internal states in an attempt to reach an adequate level of variety;

this also leads us to a self-organization dynamic where there is a transition between static and dynamic states. The state can be both a Viable System, the surroundings of smaller viable systems, and also part of a larger one.

Part 4: Recasting the Constitution

1 *Theory of the Constitution*

1.1 A Generic Model

The word *constitution* comes from the Latin *constitutio*, and although its modern conception dates from the 18th century, its origins can be traced back to ancient times. In Ancient Greece, *politeia* (Fix-Zamudio, Valencia Carmona, 2005, p. 45) was the term used to describe the structure of the communities or city states; in Rome, *res publica* was used, and *constitutio* designated the legislative acts or their consequences (*constituere iura*) (Monroy Cabra, 2005).

In legal scholarship there tends to be *three views of what the constitution is*: the *legal*, the *political* and the *cultural or sociological* perspectives. Those who uphold the first see it as a fundamental norm that organizes the state, the second is viewing it as a political order, and those akin to the third conceive of it as a set of values that comprise the state; there are, obviously, those that join two of those perspectives or even advance an amalgam of the three.

The legal view is widely known, as it has had many proponents since the rise of the modern conception of the constitution. Hauriou defines a national constitution as the statute of the state as a corporation and its members, which is established by a "constituent power" as an assembly with special legislative procedures and promulgates it in the name of a sovereign nation (Hariou, 1929, p. 242). Burdeau sees it also as the rules that legitimize the power of the sovereign (García Pelayo, 1951, p. 90).

In the American legal tradition, the constitution as a law appears in the 78th essay of *The Federalist Papers* and in *Marbury v. Madison*. In it, Judge Marshall interprets the Supremacy Clause and with it institutes judicial review, taking the supremacy of the Constitution as its fundamental principle. Leonard W. Levy summarizes: "… by 'constitution', Americans meant a supreme law creating the government, limiting it, unalterable by it, and above it" (Levy, 1986, p. 356).

A legal conception of the constitution: a) bears a norm that creates the institutions that carry out governmental functions; b) serves as a base of a legal system; c) is supreme in nature, for no act of government is above it and it has legal mechanisms that ensure that this is so; d) legitimizes political power; and e) as a law, is a factor of social coherence.

On *the political* conception, one of its most known proponents is Carl Schmitt, who has several conceptions regarding the constitution: an absolute concept which implies seeing the Supreme Law as a system; a relative notion that envisions it as a multitude of individual laws, called "constitutional laws"; a positive notion that comprehends it as a political decision; and an ideal concept that embodies a constitution that is created under certain notions of constitutionalism (separation of powers, written constitution, liberalism, etc.) (Schmitt, 2006, pp. 29, 37, 45–46, 58).

With the absolute notion of the constitution, Schmitt gives four meanings: a) a concrete situation of a polity and the social ordering of a state; b) a special way of social and political ordering (special form of domination); c) the principle of dynamic evolution of a political unit; and d) a system of norms (Schmitt, 2006, pp. 30–31, 33). The relative conception is a formal one, that is, a constitution is any law that comprises certain requirements: it is written, and its amendment procedure is complicated. That is, it is rigid.

In the positive notion of the constitution, Schmitt conceives it as a popular decision, a political will that creates the constitution which can be the product of a negotiation among political groups, but also comprises the essence of the constitution. In the first aspect, "a Constitution is valid by virtue of an existential political will from those that give it ..." The second aspect is treated as the essence or spirit of a constitution, for the fact that amendment procedures exist does not mean that there are parts of the constitution that could be freely changed (Schmitt, 2006, pp. 46, 49).

Finally, in the ideal concept Schmitt makes an exposition of the elements that comprise a constitution that is created under a rule of law: a) a system of guarantees of bourgeois liberty; b) a separation of powers; and c) a written constitution (Schmitt, 2006, pp. 59, 60, 61).

Regarding *the constitution as culture*, Professor Lucas Verdú makes a detailed exposition of what comprises it. He states his "prepositional" theory, in which the constitution is as follows: a) a fundamental law difficult to amend, that organizes and limits public powers and assures rights and liberties (concept of constitution); b) a set of "ideological, valuative and socioeconomic factors that influence the Fundamental Text and that must be proved to obtain a deeper knowledge about it" (concept about the constitution); and c) bears self-awareness, which reflects in political debate, scholarship and jurisprudence (concept in the constitution) (Verdú, 1998, pp. 47–48). For this author, when these three concepts meet in a constitution, then it can be said that it is made effective.

Another concept of importance in Lucas Verdú's scholarship is what he calls political formula, which he defines as "an ideological expression, grounded on values, normative and institutionally organized, that rests on a socioeconomic structure". He further explains that the interaction of the elements of the political formula harmonize with each other, and produce political dynamism and a constitutional sentiment – that is, a feeling of acceptance from the population (Verdú, 1998, pp. 50–51).

Constitutions are usually the highest echelon of a normative hierarchy, which can be understood as a supra-to-subordination relationship between a norm that regulates the creation of another and said created norm, the former being superior to the latter in part because it gives basis to the validity of the inferior. This is known as the supremacy principle and translates to the idea that there is no law with a superior value, and acts of authority-inclusive laws that are in contradiction to the Supreme Law are subject to annulment (Castillo del Valle 2004, p. 21).

In a standard model of the constitution there is a usage of the state's force to administer the constitution, even against the will of its subjects. This is known as *constitutional review*, which is defined by Ginsburg as "the power to examine statutes and government actions for conformity with the constitution" (Ginsburg).

Due to the fact that it is based on the principle of supremacy, *constitutional review cannot be applicable to constitutional amendments*, for its scope is circumscribed to statutes that are hierarchically inferior, and if an amendment is compliant to the procedure of reform it is incorporated into the constitution. Also, it is not possible to establish hierarchies between articles of the constitution, for the text would completely lose its coherence. Carmona Tinoco writes about a principle of non-contradiction between constitutional norms, which states that because they have the same hierarchy, two articles of supreme level cannot be considered contradictory, so they must be interpreted harmoniously (Carmona Tinoco, 1996, p. 115).

1.2 Critique

All of the definitions of a constitution have their advantages, and usually they are used in tandem; however, there is no composite model that uses legal, political and sociological definitions at the same time. In many cases, legal and political philosophers debate on the idoneity of one concept over the other, but there is a lack of a broader instance that can also serve as a reference point for policymakers.

However, most if not all of these concepts have in common the existence of a hierarchy where it reigns supreme and where constitutional review is used to revert actions and strike down laws that go against it. There needs to be a more versatile model of a constitution that can adapt to the current context, but also one that can be used in tandem with the idea of the state as a Viable System Model.

Also, the idea that there is a strict hierarchy where the constitution can only be enforced by the state is too rigid and does not fit with what takes place in political and legal practice. That is, there is no room for the voluntary application of a constitution by the citizens or by the government itself; for instance, the right of petition that most democratic states possess is used by a citizen in the first place, and only when there is a response or lack of that is not justified, we have an enforcement of said right.

Finally, in respect to the impossibility of reviewing a constitutional amendment, this does not coincide with comparative constitutional law. In his book *Judicial Review of Constitutional Amendments: A Comparative Study*, Kemal Gözler makes one of the most complete studies of constitutional review of amendments. His research coalesces in the following diagram (*Gözler, 2008*).

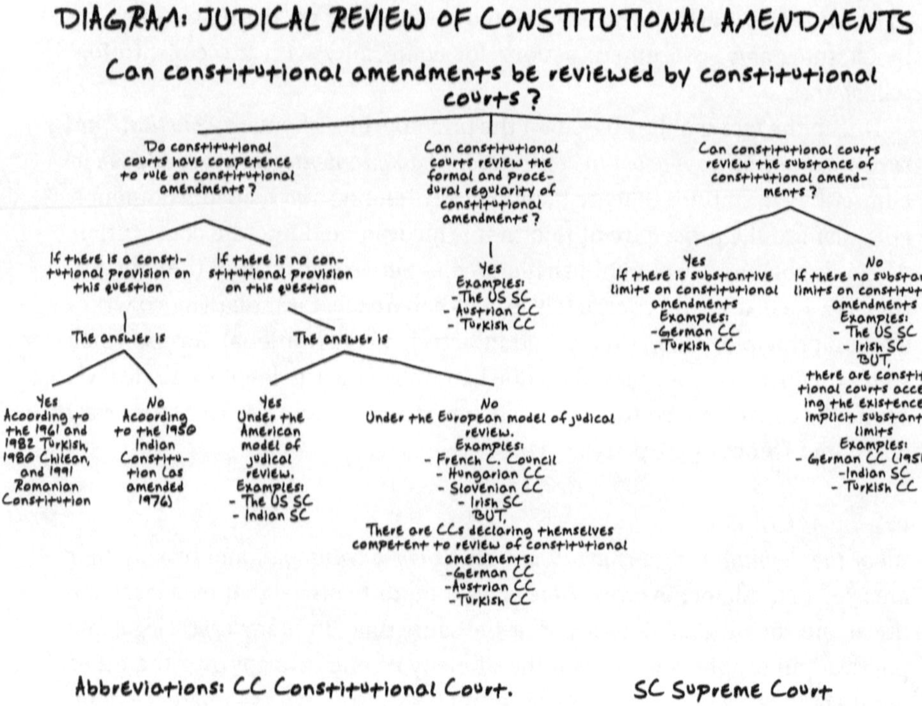

2 *An Alternative: The Constitutional Order Model*

The *constitution is then a special type of law that a state performs to create itself and its dominion over a territory*; it is self-referential because it makes mention of itself and its amendment in the text, that is, constitutional norms create themselves and give way to a legal hierarchy and a normative system. They will be defined as a composite project of reality that encompasses legal, political, sociological, economic and historical elements.

Legal norms in general are projects of reality, that is, hypothetical realities (an Ought) that are to take place by means of their application by agents when there is a factual situation that satisfices its requirements. Although the norm is expressed by means of a legal hypothesis, which is contingent, the sole fact that it is stated in a physical medium and transmitted to individuals so they may know of it generates a change by itself.

This means that the sole action that seeks to change reality, even if it does not achieve its purpose, affects it by means of its own existence as the latter will adapt to it. A constitution is also a project that gives way to others and conditions their content by means of its continued existence; to manifest into reality, the constitution will be subject to application and interpretation.

The idea of the project of reality is flexible, and it purports to be, and because of this, one can configure the theory of the constitution in many ways. My take on what comprises the constitution as a composite project of reality will be as follows:

A constitution is the product of a bargain between political elites. This idea is sustained among others, by Elkins et al. and by Russell Hardin, and is explained in the context of coordination theory in a note on counterinsurgency and constitutional design in the *Harvard Law Review*. It states that constitutions should not be understood as contracts, but as bargains among competing groups. This sets out a "coordination dilemma" which consists of society's need for institutional structures that coordinate basic functions. Therefore, as they compete, political elites develop a stable governance structure which is approved by all (Harvard Law Review).

These notions on coordination and constitutive bargaining processes dispel the classic notion that the constitution is a systematized body. This cannot be due to the fact that agreement between groups may lead to general terms that can be interpreted broadly, to them deciding not to address certain issues or to contradicting articles within the constitutional text.

In their book, Elkins et al. also analyze the factors that allow constitutions to endure, among these being inclusiveness, that is, the capacity of a constitutive process to allow intervention by public opinion. When this is the case, a constitution fits into the fiction that is the product of popular will, and in this case it is a constitutional decision. This fiction – inclusiveness as a popular decision – can be used as the main legitimizing principle of the constitution (and with it, the whole legal system) in what Hans Kelsen called a Basic Norm (*Grundnorm* in German). The Basic Norm seeks to explain legality and normativity of law, and does so in the form of a presupposition of the legal validity of the (first, historical) constitution of the relevant legal system (Stanford Encyclopedia of Philosophy, The Pure Theory of Law).

The legitimacy of a constitution can stem from the negotiation process but by itself is imperfect: it is the popular participation that perfects such legitimacy and endows upon said bargain the fiction of a popular decision, and as such, institutes itself as the legitimizing force of the legal system. This is a circular process: the constitution subsists as long as it is applied and believed in by those who are ruled by it; this takes place as a set of continuous feedback loops that only come to a stop when there is a total collapse in the constitutional order.

Now, the negotiation process gives birth to a norm that is of supreme hierarchy. This supremacy does not mean it is a fundamental norm, for there can be statutes that predate the constitution and that are in vigor in the legal system. The concept of a fundamental norm entails that every norm has a source they emanate from. If there is not a unique source, then *a constitution is a conditioning norm*, that is, its content conditions the existence of laws that bear lesser hierarchy. Returning to the *3 by 3 by 3 model*, we can see that *the constitution forms part of a heterarchy*.

History is an important factor that determines the content of a constitution. It helps shape the bargaining process, for past events influence the desires of the negotiating groups. For example, the Spanish Constitution of 1978 has a broad Bill of Rights in reaction to what was lived by the population under the dictatorial regime of Francisco Franco. A second example is the Mexican Constitution of 1917, which was the first in the world to implement social rights in reaction to the oppression and repression that workers and farmers endured under the dictatorship of Porfirio Díaz. Social values and principles are also reflected in the bargaining process, as values and principles permeate into the constitutional text and shape the institutions that emanate from it.

The conditioning norm brings about an institutional structure, which is made of political, legal and economic elements. The political aspect comprises the dynamics that ensue from the distribution of power, how it is exercised and how it can be accessed. The economic aspect is concerned with the perception and distribution of the resources of the *state*. And finally, the legal aspect is the rules and structuring of social behavior, which includes the economic and political aspects and can extend to every other aspect of life in society.

The combination of legal and economic aspects comprises the regulation of perception and distribution of resources, and the funding of the legal structure and its enforcement, while the merger between the political and legal elements deals with the regulation of power dynamics and the political process of the creation of norms. All of this can be summarized in the following diagram:

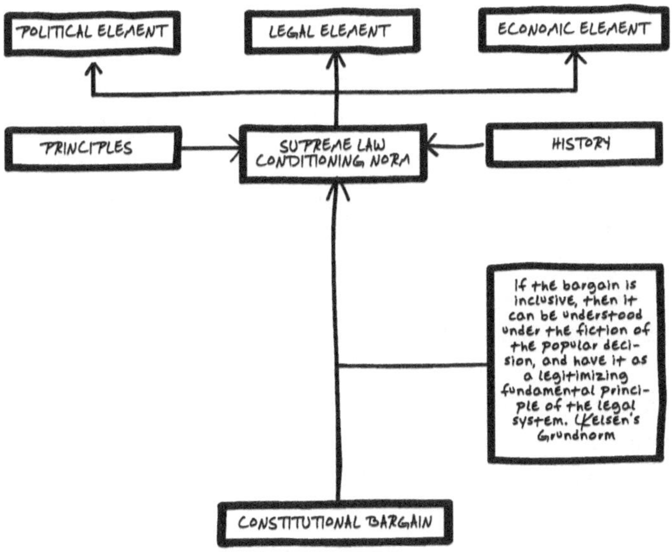

As a legal norm, *the constitution has an endonorm*, which comprises its logical structure and can have ontic, deontic and technical norms; *and a perinorm*, which comprises the socio-political rules that surround it and the morality implied in its content, acceptance and application (Mancilla, 2015). The latter will be defined as the action of putting something into operation. Constitutional application is the way in which the Supreme Law is made effective, which encompasses three different aspects:

- *Efficiency*: Comprises the ways in which a constitution can be made effective. We talk about a coactive constitutional application when the state's force is used to enforce the constitution, and voluntary application when the government and citizens make it effective without using legitimate strength. This aspect has its foundation in the principle of constitutional supremacy, which is both the idea that the constitution must be the justification of other norms and that it has a superior value.
- *Congruence*: Describes the harmonic relation that the constitution must have with its own principles; this means that coactive and voluntary acts of application must follow the principles stated by the Supreme Law, and not only do so in the letter of the law. It also means that if a constitution is ever changed (this is also a voluntary act), it must follow the spirit of the constitution; otherwise, the force of the state could be used to review the change that was made.
- *Efficacy*: Entails the subjects over whom the effects of the act of application take place, which include *individuals and mobile legal persons*, and *geographical persons*, both of whom are also divided at the same time into two.

In the case of geographical persons, there are those that have direct relation with the act of authority and those that have indirect relation. In the same way, people and mobile persons can be divided into those that have a direct and indirect relationship with the application of the constitution.

As we saw in the *3 by 3 by 3 model*, if a fact matches the hypothesis of a legal norm, it must be applied, and this act entails an interpretation, an informal change or an amendment. In constitutional law, there are three acts that can take place:

- *Constitutional interpretation*: As defined by Brest, it "... comprehends the methods or strategies available to people attempting to resolve disputes about the meaning or application of the Constitution" (Brest, 1986, p. 464). The purpose of interpretation is to fill a deficiency in the law by means of extending the signification of the legal text; when a void in the law is to be filled but there is no norm to interpret, then the activity to be made is that of gap-filling.
- *Constitutional resistance*: Francisco Tomás y Valiente defines it as the adaptability to the political dynamic that a constitution can have; it also entails a capacity of being interpreted in a flexible manner, and changing in its function in response to new problems and sensibilities, making amendment unnecessary. It consists of assimilating, without leaving out, the different political expectations not opposed frontally to its text, which translates to a capacity to assume mutations (Tomás y Valiente).
- *Constitutional mutation*: Jellinek defines it as "that modification of the constitution that leaves its text unchanged, without formal amendment that is produced by facts that do not have to be followed by the intention or conscience of such mutation" (author's translation) (Dau-Lin, 1998, p. 29). This is what I have referred to before as informal change.

Constitutional interpretation and resistance are similar in substance because they are constitutional coping mechanisms for the diverse circumstances that influence the duration of a constitution. They differ in the fact that interpretation can expand the meaning of the Supreme Law as long as the norm permits it, but the nature of resistance is adaptability to change, and though it overlaps in some terrains with interpretation, it can prescind from it and border with gap-filling. Regarding the interception of interpretation and resistance, there is a type of constitutional interpretation that Sagüés calls mutative interpretation, which is an interpretative process that admits the existence of a mutation (Sagüés, 2007).

The concepts of interpretation, resistance and mutation comprise what Elkins et al. call flexibility, that is, the capacity of a constitution to endure and be applied; this entails adaptation to and the incorporation of external stimuli (which can be economic, legal, political, the passage of time, among others) into its structure, ranging from expanding its meaning to changing it altogether (Elkins, Ginsburg, Melton, 2009, pp. 81–82). *Interpretation, resistance and mutation are degrees of constitutional flexibility.*

The fulfilling of the hypotheses of the constitution and its application, yielding interpretation, resistance and mutation are *constitutional interactions*: acts made within the state-constitution dynamic that result in the approaching or repelling between the social reality and the projected reality. This can be expressed graphically in the following way:

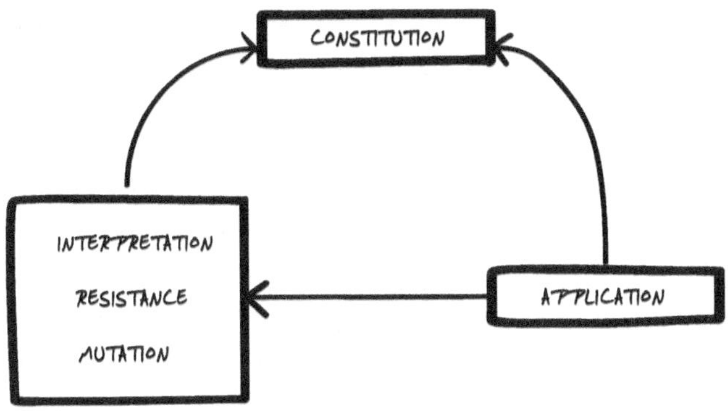

A *constitutional order* is the sum of all of these interactions, which take place in constant and continuous cycles that broaden in parts and restrict in others the content and meaning of a constitution. This forms a system that is part of others that are encompassed in the functioning of the state (as a Viable System Model), and it helps the latter to reconfigure itself if needed.

Part 5: Recasting the Separation of Powers

1 *Separation of Powers*

1.1 A Generic Model

The concept of *separation of powers* has some roots in ancient ideology, with the idea of a mixed government emanating from Greek thought, with authors such as Herodotus, Plato, and Aristotle, among others, and was subsequently picked up by medieval scholars such as Thomas Aquinas, Marsilius of Padua and Machiavelli (Fix-Zamudio, Valencia Carmona, 2005, pp. 405, 406). In his book *The Spirit of the Laws*, Montesquieu advances the concept of the separation of powers, taking as a base Locke's liberalism and his dichotomy of the legislative-executive (Claus, 2004).

This book was the product of 20 years of work and first saw the light in 1748 by means of an anonymous publication. It had a pervasive impact on political thought, especially on the founding generation of the United States of America. In writing this book, Montesquieu traveled to England between 1729 and 1731, and attempted to describe the British constitutional system.

To him there were three powers in every government: the power to create laws (which included enactment, amendment and abrogation); the power to execute laws under international and domestic law; and the power of judging, which emanated from the application under national law, regarding the resolving of disputes and criminal punishment. The first power was exercised by the Houses of Parliament, the second by the judge, and the third by juries (Claus, 2004).

When the separation of powers got to the United States, the exercise of the power of judging was entrusted not only to juries, but to a Judiciary branch, which was an arrangement very different from that which had prevailed in England. Unlike the French in 1791, the American Founding Fathers had a different understanding of the separation of powers – that is, their conception was not rigid, but had a dynamic distribution of power. To James Madison, Montesquieu (Claus, 2004):

> ... did not mean that these departments ought to have no *partial agency* in, or no *control* over the acts of each other. His meaning, as his own words import, and still more conclusively as illustrated by the example in his eye [namely, Britain], can amount to no more than this, that where the *whole* power of one department is exercised by the same hands which possessed the *whole* power of another department, the fundamental principles of a free constitution are subverted.

In an attempt to create distance between historical conceptions and form an abstract model upon which to build, the notions advanced by Italian scholar Costantino Mortati are useful. To him, *separation of powers is a principle consisting of correlated organs, differently formed, independent from one another, and with their own set of competences which are identified as key functions of the state*: to legislate, to administrate, and to impart justice. He states five conditions for its application (Mortati, 1969, p. 371):

- Determining the competence of the organs of each power based on the material content of actions belonging to the various functions.

- The allocation of each group of functions in favor of those of bodies regarded as better suited, by virtue of their composition to adopt them with maximum satisfaction of public interest.
- The independence of each power regarding others, in order to be able to preserve the autonomy of operation of each.
- The typicality of the forms necessary for the enactment of actions belonging to each of the functions.
- The particular effectiveness of the actions attributed to each function in correspondence with the assigned practical end.

In the United States there is a *doctrinal division of the separation of powers* between two currents: *formalism and functionalism*. The first conceives three departments upon which governmental tasks are divided, while the second states that these separate powers have shared and overlapping functions.

Magill states that the difference between both competing conceptions of separation of powers is akin to that between rules and standards: to formalism, any structural question is to be resolved by means of referring to the text of the constitution, while for functionalism, these problems are solved by means of recurring to a series of postulates (Magill, 2001, pp. 603, 607–610). To put it in other terms: formalism advocates for a static distribution of capacity, but for functionalism, this distribution is dynamic. Formalism can be illustrated in the following way:

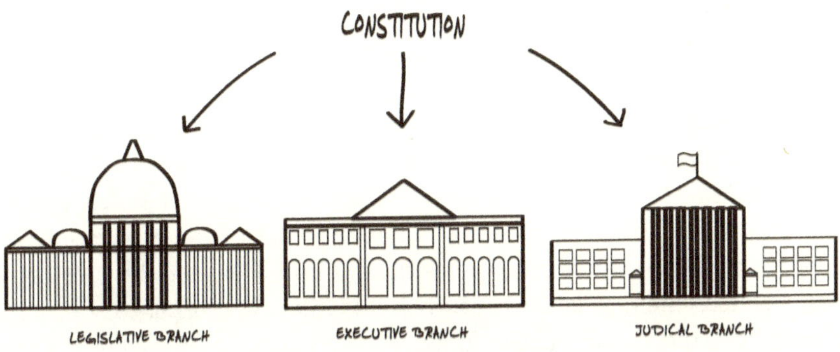

While functionalism is visually represented in this manner:[15]

15 Taken and modified from the personal webpage of Professor Pedro A. Malavet of University of Florida Law School, Comparative Law, Class Notes Part 11, http://nersp.nerdc.ufl.edu/~malavet/comparat/notes/new11.htm.

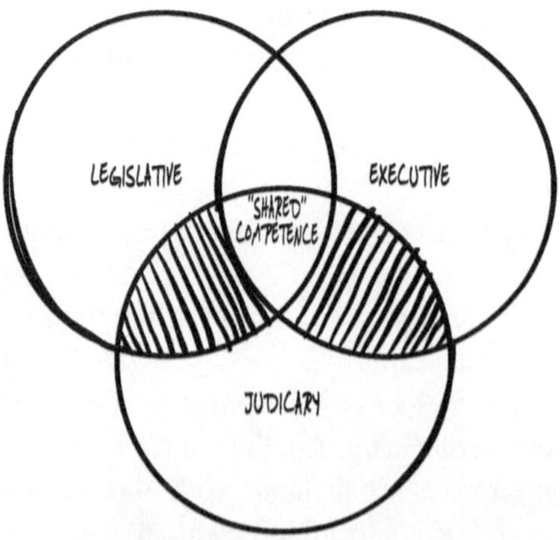

Despite the constant debate between proponents of both currents, there are some similarities among both – for example, both look to disperse the functions of government among the existing institutions, and coincide in that power must be divided among the legislative, executive and judicial. Magill articulates the points of consensus (Magill, 2000, pp. 1127, 1154):

> First ... the system of separation of powers is intended to prevent a single governmental institution from possessing and exercising too much power. Second, courts and commentators also basically, though not universally, agree on the mechanisms by which that objective is to be achieved.

One of the many problems of formalism is that it depends upon the distinction between each branch of power, and there is no consensus among scholars in this regard (Magill, 2001, pp. 612–614). To this, Madison recognized in Federalist No. 37: "Experience has instructed us that no skill in the science of government has yet been able to discriminate and define, with sufficient certainty, its three great provinces, the Legislative, Executive and Judiciary" (Magill, 2001, p. 614). On the other hand, the problem of functionalism is that by conceiving it as the balance of power between branches, proper criteria for such distribution of power must be issued (Magill, 2001, pp. 626–627).

1.2 Critique

Both formalism and functionalism denote a problem of separation of powers – there is no basic criteria by which the allocation of power can be made between branches. In the case of formalism there is no method to empirically determine the ideal way to distinguish one branch from the other along with the functions they must perform, as many states have different configurations of the competences of their branches; with functionalism there is no way to determine the correct "balance" of power.

Because it seeks to constrain the distribution of powers into a typology in which either there are three "ideal" sectors, or in which there needs to be a "balance" between the functions carried out by them when there are many ways to structure the usage of capacity, the concept of separation of powers can be considered as too rigid to adapt to constant changes.

Because social systems are prone to change, a rigid typology is not enough to guarantee a distribution of power; that is, *there can be no universal formula.* Magill drives this point home when she asks: "Is it possible to devise an approach to separation of powers that does not depend on distinguishing among the powers of government and treating the branches as entities that must be balanced with one another?" (Magill, 2001, p. 649) We have, then, that the separation of powers model does not entirely adapt to society's needs as new government functions have surfaced in the light of those which do not fit within the frame of the three functions.

Laurence Claus, in his article "Montesquieu's Mistakes and the True Meaning of Separation" adduces that in crafting his model of separation of powers by observing the British constitutional system he misunderstood the English common law and the doctrine of precedent. Montesquieu inherited from his uncle the office of the *président à mortier* of the Parliament of Bordeaux, which was mainly an adjudicative body, and while acting in this capacity, he formed a perception of adjudication as fact-finding and application of the law (Claus, 2004):

> When Montesquieu spoke of judicial power, or rather, of the "power of judging," he meant a function wholly shorn of lawmaking potential. It was fact-finding, a precursor to the execution of existing law. When Montesquieu spoke of the legislative power, he meant the power to make law, by whomever held. But resolving disputes may require judicial exposition of existing law. Exposition is elaboration. Elaboration is lawmaking ...

This mistake in his conception of the British common law and political system means that by overlooking the fact that judges make rules by means of precedent, his model of separation of powers is flawed from its origin: in delineating the functions of each power, rulemaking and adjudication sometimes conflate.

Loewenstein centers his criticism on the fact that specialization and division of labor became necessary for organs of government to perform their duties, and that this originated as a liberal response to absolutism: "the power addressees are better off if these activities are performed by different organs: freedom is the ideological telos of the separation doctrine ... Only liberal constitutionalism identified individual liberty with the separation of 'powers.'" (Loewenstein, 1965, p. 36). He also considers that separation of powers is not essential to the functioning of the political system and that as a term it is antiquated, and therefore should be denominated as *separation of functions*: "What is colloquially, if erroneous, spoken as separation of powers is operationally only the distribution of specific state functions among different state organs" (Loewenstein, 1965, p. 36).

Rubin's criticism is framed more towards the reality of the modern administrative state, in which the size of the central administration is disproportionate to the other branches, and the fact that the metaphor of branches does not give a realistic image of the interaction that occurs among governmental organs (Rubin, 2005, p. 46). Also, he states that the branches metaphor ignores the need for political control: "... which is crucial in the modern state, involves a dynamic interaction among different parts of government that the three-branch does not illuminate" (Rubin, 2005, pp. 45–47).

Regarding civil law scholarship and their criticism, García Roca acknowledges that there have been great changes in separation of powers since the time when this model was conceived, and although his perspective comes from Spanish law, it is applicable in legal systems of civil law tradition and also to the administrative state. This author makes a list that is relevant to this study (García Roca, 2000):

- There have appeared new organs, different from the classic triad of powers (with the Constitutional Tribunal and the Crown cited as examples).
- Traditional branches have been reconfigured and are different from the composition envisioned by liberal constitutionalism.
- New auxiliary organs of the branches have appeared, and some of them have constitutional relevance.
- There have appeared new functions, different from the classical ones.

In this context, it is useful to introduce the civil law concept of extra branch organs (*organos extrapoder*), which are defined as: "the state organs not situated within the scope of any of the three classic powers of the State (Legislative, Executive, Judiciary)" (Sagüés, 2007). These organs fit into many of the changes that García Roca has described: they are organs outside the branch triad, some of them can be auxiliary to the branches, and they can exercise functions different from those of the three powers.

Another similar concept – though not identical – is that of autonomous constitutional organs (*órganos constitucionales autónomos*), which are organs that have autonomy by means of constitutional mandate. This idea can overlap in some parts with that of extra branch organs, but they cannot be auxiliary to branches, and unlike the other organs, can only exist by virtue of their express creation by a constitution.

2 *An Alternative: The Distribution of Functions Model*

To replace the separation of powers, we propose a model we call *distribution of functions*. Rubin, seeking to substitute the antiquated branch model, proposes to base the relationships of governmental organs in the image of networks. He divides this schematic into hardware and software, the first being the way that the network is organized, and the second, the types of operations that are carried out in this structure (Rubin, 2005, pp. 50–51).

On the hardware level he defines it as a set of interconnections between different "units", which are "a region where matter, energy, or information is generated or altered for transmission through an interconnection" (Rubin, 2005, p. 49). Within the architecture of the network as a frame of government, Rubin distinguishes several levels of observation (Rubin, 2005, p. 49):

1. Individual human beings (lowest level)
2. Offices: physical locations where groups of individuals work in daily contact
3. Departments of agencies
4. The agencies themselves and other units that are defined as separate entities
5. Nation-states or associated groups of nation-states (highest level)

This framework is applicable to all the organs of government, whether they are within the "branches" or outside them; all of them can generate and exchange information and resources when carrying out their respective functions. In developing the network model as software, Rubin describes the operation of each unit, which can also be known as *design or operational scope*: "a region where matter, energy, or information is generated or altered for transmission through an interconnection" (Rubin, 2005, pp. 51–53).

Taking into account what we said in Part 2 about the Viable System Model and variety management, the hardware aspect can be understood as the former and the software as the latter. This is not incompatible with the idea of networks, as they are a way to conceptualize social structures, and one could visualize an organ of government as a network and then color or mark its components as part of one of the systems of the VSM. For instance, in this visualization of the Executive Branch of the United States of America during the early Obama presidency, made by Jessica Lipnack, we have the following organization:[16]

16 Taken from https://endlessknots.netage.com/.a/6a00df3523b1d08834010536e4dcf9970b-pi; found in: http://crtunnard.blogspot.com/2011/09/social-network-analysis-in-obama.html.

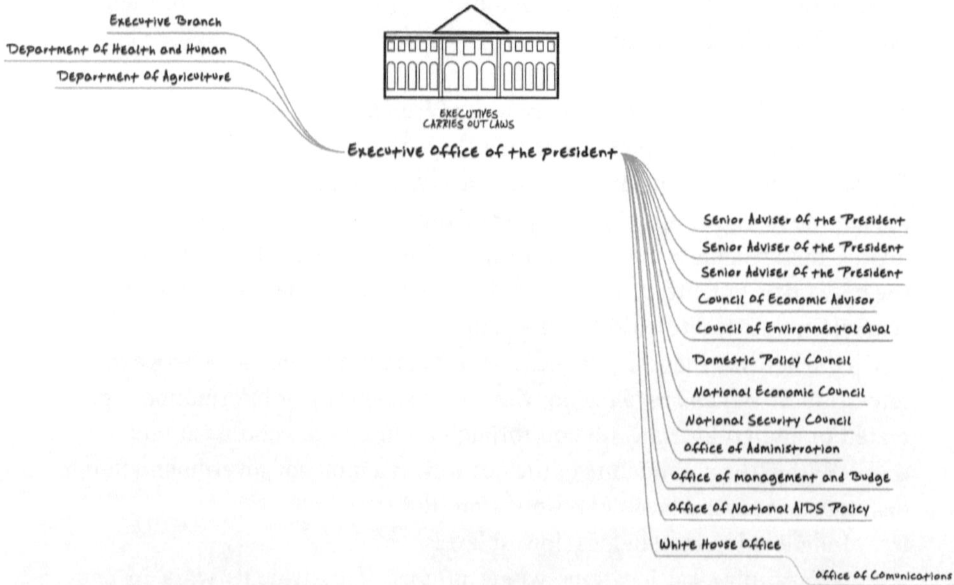

Of that, we can form the following Viable System Model:

- *System 1*: The population that receives the policies of the Executive Branch is what constitutes the implementation aspect of the VSM, and thus it comprises this system.
- *System 2*: The different offices that seek to detect and correct the immediate oscillations of implementing the policies on the population.
- *System 3*: The Executive Office of the President, headed by the Chiefs of Staff, handles the day-to-day of the Executive. Senior advisers and other specialists may act as a System 3*.
- *System 4*: The President and the Cabinet are those in charge of the planning.
- *System 5*:[17] The President, Chiefs of Staff and the different Senior Advisors Offices may respond to social mobilizations, political groups and parties, and groups that act as intelligentsias, and thus determine the identity of the Executive Branch.

This example tells us that the Executive Branch is structured as an ego-centric network; however, the conjunction of the three branches and other autonomous organs may yield a socio-centric network, and there may be nodes that act as brokers between all of them. Thus, network theory is a valuable tool in

17 Eden Medina notes in her book *Cybernetic Revolutionaries* that in the first meeting between Stafford Beer and Salvador Allende, in the effort to organize the nationalized Chilean economy as a VSM, the latter conceived System 5 as the people. See page 75.

obtaining a broad perspective of the social organization of the exercise of the state's power.

Loewenstein suggests a new division of the functions trilogy: policy determination, policy execution and policy control. The first "refers to the major choices of policy the state community is called to make …" (Loewenstein, 1965, p. 43); the second "is the instrumentality for the implementation of the policy decisions …" (Loewenstein, 1965, p. 46); while the third consists in political responsibility, and "is the situation in which a specific power holder is accountable, for the conduct of the function assigned to him, to another power holder …" (Loewenstein, 1965, p. 50).

Loewenstein and Rubin's positions are complements: policy determination, execution and control can be framed within the software model of a network. This can also be considered in terms of variety: the determination of policy is the pondering of the perceived variety of the system vis-à-vis that of the environment, which is also influenced by the existing variety of the VSM. Put in simple terms, it is seeing what I can do (internal variety) to address a problem (external variety), with my capacity of doing things being the limit of my perception (internal variety).

The execution consists of matching the perceived variety of the environment (here comprised by a problem to be solved and the resistance to the proposed measures) with the internal variety of the VSM; control is the restating of the measures determined, or course correction after seeing that the variety used was adequate, not adequate, or partially so.

The distribution of functions model reinterprets the approach towards existing governmental organs within a political system. There would be organs like the Judiciary that would be a small network by themselves, and organs that exist individually and do not exist within a hierarchy scheme, and others that would depend on one or more organs. Instead of performing administrative, legislative or judicial functions, the activities of each organ would have to be considered under the schema of policy creation, implementation and control, with some organs carrying out one or more of these functions.

The dynamic nature of the distribution of functions can be analogized to a house retrofitted to withstand an earthquake. Instead of being a fixed structure that lies upon a moving base, the distribution of functions adapts to the political dynamic of the state and minimizes the frictions and tensions that such social changes entail. This example can be developed further by the analysis of the following video set in the footnote.[18]

18 Youtube, *Earthquake Protective Foundation – base isolation video*, Available at: http://www.youtube.com/watch?v=ChaqMDc4ces&feature=related. (Accessed, January 20, 2020).

In it, two structures are put on a movable base. The one on the left is made on a regular foundation, while the one on the right was built on an Earthquake Protective Foundation. As the movement continues in the video, the building on the left looks more affected, while the one on the right barely moves. This is the same case with the separation of powers and the distribution of functions models: the first is too rigid and does not adapt easily to the changes in the distribution of power, due to the fact that it cannot have a fixed standard that can exemplify how power must be dispersed; while the second, because it is more fluid, adapts better to these movements.

This happens because of cybernetics: All organs in the distribution of functions have different tasks to perform, and they might be more important than others in certain moments or contexts; that is, this model is a heterarchy. Also, they communicate and feedback with each other, either to work together or to check on one another.

Part 6: Recasting the Public/Private Distinction

1 *The Public/Private Distinction*

1.1 A Generic Model

The *arbitrariness of public/private as a category needs to be anchored in a sociohistorical context*, for its knowledge helps us to determine the scope and limitations of the category and ascertain if a change is needed. The roots of the public/private distinction can be found in the two fragments of the *Corpus Juris Civilis* which are attributed to Ulpian: the "public" is found in the *Institutes* and defined as "*quod ad statum rei romanae spectat,*" while the "private" is found in the *Digest* as "*quod ad singulorum utilitatem*" (Bobbio, 1989, p. 11). These fragments are taken by medieval commentators and consolidate in the following formula: "public law refers to the expectations of the Roman republic and private to the utility of an individual" (Sohm).

Horwitz states that the distinction came to be from the development of the notions of the nation-state and sovereignty in the 17th century, and as a reaction to the efforts of monarchs and legislators to wield unrestrained law-making power. The creation of a private sphere free of state intervention and control came to be a power-limiting effort. In the 19th century the public/private became a central point in American legal and political theory, as the market became a main institution of legitimization. As a way of creating an understanding of Law devoid of politics, scholars strived to make a clear-cut distinction between public law and private law, and subsequently a neutral system of doctrine (Horwitz, 1982, pp. 1423–1425).

The perceived content of the public/private distinction is variable, but I will form a generic model of this distinction by making use of Continental constitutional law textbooks, which tend to compile existing theories about the nature of the public/private distinction. Naranjo gathers three criteria for differentiating public from private law (Naranjo Mesa, 2006, pp. 12–14):

- *Social organization*: Public is distinguished from private as the government is from the governed.
- *The nature of the norm*: Public is separated from private by means of the interests that its rules protect; the collective vis-à-vis the individual.
- *The procedures that are used to create the rules*: Whereas public law is created as a set of coercive rules that can be subject to sanction, private law features principles of contract law and the principle of party autonomy.

Although important, none of these factors can construct a meaningful separation between public and private, and because they are in constant flow, they can be used to both partially or wholly reconstruct the distinction. That is, social organization, norms nor procedures can yield a substantive notion of the public/private distinction; rather, a skeleton can be the subject of debate and controversy, and can yield easily to one conclusion or another, as noted by Klare (1982).[19] This means that a model of the distinction needs to instead be centered on the actors that partake in the distinction and their behavior.

Following this lead, the most widespread doctrine on how to separate public from private attends to the nature of the legal relations that take place between different actors, which can be of two types (Naranjo Mesa, 2006, p. 13):

- *Coordination*: The intervening subjects act as equals – for example, individuals that interact with one another in a commercial transaction, private citizens and states when the latter does not act as a sovereign, and the relationship between organs of the state.
- *Subordination*: The intervening subjects are not equals – rather, one is superior to the other. A prime example of this is the state when it acts as a sovereign.

When there is a relationship of coordination, where individuals act as equals in the pursuit of their interests, one is within the realm of private law. When there is one of subordination, where the state acts in a superior-to-subordinate relationship – characterized by coercion and coaction – regarding the individuals that comprise it, one is within public law. Further criteria of distinction include: a) public law being heteronomous and imperative, and private law

19 In his article "Public/Private Distinction in Labor Law" in the *Pennsylvania Law Review*, Klare explains the way in which the public/private distinction can be used as an ideological weapon.

being more about mediation and arbitration in solving conflicts; and b) public law favoring the collective interest, while private law the interest of individuals (Naranjo Mesa, 2006, p. 13).

This seemingly orderly relation has been objected to on the grounds that there can be unequal relationships in public law, which brings forth a third type of relationship, *equalization*, where a third party intervenes to balance an unequal relation (Fix-Zamudio and Valencia Carmona, 2005, pp. 15–16). Instances of this can be found in the struggles that gave way to the Mexican Constitution of 1917, which was the first to enshrine social rights.

All these relationships presuppose two kinds of acting parties: a) a territorial entity, such as a city, a region or a state, which enacts coercive rules over its territory; and b) individuals and groups that can band together to achieve a purpose and have a set of rules that they enact over one another. This set of rules is not necessarily impressed over a territory, as sophisticated groups can have a presence in several designations (Mancilla; 2017).

Furthermore, this model functions with traditional notions of power that presuppose a relationship or series of relationships in which one party imposes their will, despite the opposition of others. Loewenstein defines it within the lines of a reciprocal socio-psychological relationship operating between those who hold and exercise power, and those towards whom it is directed (Loewenstein, 1965, p. 6). Lasswell and Kaplan regard power as participation in the creation of policy decisions that involve severe sanctions, which are to be used to sustain it against opposition (Lasswell, Kaplan, 1951, pp. 74–75).

Under this schema there is a marked division between both that seems very intuitive: Government is the entity that solely exercises coercion and all of its actions are focused on procuring benefits for the public, while private persons can seek to achieve their individualized interests and ambitions, chiefly among them the pursuit of wealth. This means that there is a "public" function largely comprised of subordination and equalization relationships, while there is a "private" function made out of coordination relations.

The public/private distinction is then based on determining a "function" that categorizes behavior that can change or vary in its nature; that is, the composition of the relations that compose each (coordination, subordination and equalization) is not fixed. In general, it is understood that Government will run public services like prisons, healthcare systems, armies, and the legal system, among others, while private individuals and corporations lead productive activities in their pursuit of profit.

This latter activity also presupposes that what is private is not as harmful or dangerous as the endeavors of public actors, which are under close scrutiny and vigilance. It also presupposes that those that lead private organisms are not exactly exercising power as in the public sphere, and are only answerable to themselves. These notions, although presented here in extreme forms, permeate in varying degrees through different political structures and doctrines.

The understanding of the public/private distinction differs greatly from what scholars argue to what is stated within national constitutions, as countries have determined through political processes what counts as "public" and what as "private," with movements from the former to the latter being known as "privatization" and the inverse known as "nationalization."

Beyond the types of relationships that can take place on the public/private continuum, there is also an interest that is being pursued. In the "public" there are subordination relations and a collective interest to be achieved or protected; in the "private" there are coordination relations and an individual (or group) interest. However, in tune with the third division, the "social" has equalizing relations that look to protect or accomplish the interests of a vulnerable group (Trueba Urbina, 1951, p. 49).

Subordination presupposes the superiority of one party over the other; coordination, the equality of the interacting parties; and equalization departs from inequality and aspires to level the field between the parties (Trueba Urbina, 1951, p. 49).

What is considered public as opposed to private is both a form of understanding and a systemization of political and social relations, but it can also be used as the arena of political action, and a rhetorical device. Thus, it is neither absolute nor neutral.

1.2 Critique

Because *concepts and categories are constructions made by humans living in a social setting*, they are the product of a socio-historical setting. As such, we can conclude that the public/private distinction is made for a specific type of social system: To Horwitz, the descriptive usefulness of the public/private distinction would be circumscribed to "a society and economy of relatively small, decentralized, nongovernmental units." (Horwitz, 1982, p. 1428).

He notes that at the turn of the 19th century, private and public power conflated with widespread large-scale corporate concentration; furthermore, legal realist philosophers attacked this distinction because they perceived private institutions were encroaching upon a coercive power which had been understood as being reserved for governments (Horwitz, 1982, p. 1428).

The *substantive content of the public/private cannot be established in a clear-cut distinction*, as many phenomena can be understood either as public or private; also, one can depart from an identical premise about the public or private nature of a phenomenon and arrive at opposing conclusions (Klare,

1982, pp. 1359–1360). *This leads to an indefinite or malleable substance that is constantly recast, with ideological contests taking place over who determines the content of each iteration* (Mancilla, 2017).

An example of how public and private fluctuate can be found in the subcontracting of functions that were considered as belonging to states. For instance, in the United States there has been an increase in the outsourcing of military tasks, which range from "logistical support to military deployments/ operations, maintenance of weapons systems, protection of premises, close protection of persons, training of military and police forces at home or abroad, intelligence gathering and analysis, custody and interrogation of prisoners and, on some occasions, participation in combat" (International Committee of the Red Cross). Under the public/private distinction, this endeavor poses many problems, one of which is the application of international public law and namely, international humanitarian law.

Another example concerns the privatization of prisons in the United States, which began to thrive in the 1980s under the Reagan and Bush I presidencies, and reached its apex with Clinton, whose plan for instituting cuts in the federal workforce resulted in the contracting of private prison corporations for the incarceration of undocumented workers and high-security inmates. Currently, these types of prisons are very profitable businesses, as about 18 corporations guard 10,000 prisoners in 27 states. Private prisons receive a guaranteed amount of money for each prisoner, independent of what it costs to maintain each one (Centre for Research on Globalization).

As for the relations that constitute the public/private distinction, these also cannot be separated. States can engage in subordination as the party that is submitting; they can engage in coordination both with the state and with individuals, and can be equalizers, but also equalized themselves when they are before more powerful states (or corporations). Conversely, individuals and groups can engage with the subordination of states and other individuals or groups (like consumers); coordination can take place among the state and powerful corporations, and the latter can act as equalizers in the absence of the state (Mancilla, 2017).

States and multinational corporations can be on equal footing in economic terms, and this muddles the triad of subordination-coordination-equalization relations. For instance, the revenue of many corporations has surpassed the GDP of several countries: For the year 2010, Apple had a revenue of $65.23 billion, while Ecuador had a GDP of $58.91 billion, and Microsoft surpassed Croatia $62.48 billion to $60.59 (*Business Insider*). Another example of the muddling of the public/private distinction can be found in the German constitutional law doctrine of Third Party Effect (*Drittwirkung*), which holds that the constitution can entail legal obligations for private law interactions between private persons (Engle 2009) (Mancilla, 2017).

Furthermore, the interests of an individual or a group, those of a protected group and even those of a theoretical collective are intimately interrelated and thus cannot be easily boxed into "public", "private" or "social" (Naranjo Mesa, 2006, pp. 12–13). That is, there is no "objective" or "universal" private nor public law (Mancilla, 2017).

2 *An Alternative Model: The Mobile/Geographic Distinction*[20]

The model that I have created in this study does not make a distinction between public and private, or between state and non-state actors; rather, it *operates on the basis of between-corporate legal persons*. A new classification of legal persons will be offered to the reader, based on mobility of physical position and resources, classifying them as either *mobile* or *geographically-based* (Mancilla, 2017).

The first are comprised of the entities that can change their location between territories, or those that can be in several at once, and the second are those that base themselves in a territory and create within it a set of coercive rules. Both of these types of actors can engage in subordination, coordination and equalization relationships either with actors of their same type or with those which are different (geographical-geographical; mobile-mobile; geographical-mobile) (Mancilla, 2017).

Mobile actors are comprised by the following elements: the individual, small groups, organization, organizational set, organizational population, organizational field and world system. Geographical actors are comprised by: community, city, region/federative entity, state, confederacy of states and world system. This distinction is more focused on the interrelation between the spatial structuration of social systems and subjectivity (Mancilla, 2012; Mancilla 2017).

The *individual* is the smallest unit in the subjective set of analysis – they are a speech act-performing, reflexive animal who creates a social construct by means of continued interaction with their fellows, but at the same time is shaped by it (Mancilla, 2012; Mancilla 2017).

---

20 This idea was first developed as levels of social analyses in my article "Introduction to Sociocybernetics Part 2: Power, Culture and Institutions" in the *Journal of Sociocybernetics*. I then refined it as a model in my article "Rethinking Constitutionalism: Using Epistemology to Show the Inadequacy of the Public/Private Distinction" in *Global Jurist*.

Small groups (1 to 20 members) and *organizations* (20+) can have a broad variety of purposes and can range from highly formalized to informal agreements. An *organizational set* refers to the relationship that an organization has with other subjects based on their identity – for example, an organization will have a different relationship with its competitors, its customer, its suppliers and the government (Mancilla, 2012; Mancilla 2017).

The *organizational population* comprises all organizations that are alike in some way. They compete for the same resources, have the same interests, face the same pressures and uncertainties, and look to one another for ideas (Scott, Davis, 2007, pp. 116–117). An *organizational field* is a set of different types of organizations that engage in competitive and cooperative relations, all of which have a common set of rules and meaning systems (Powell, DiMaggio, 1991, pp. 64–65).

A *community* can be defined as a group of people that live within the same area in which they satisfy many of their needs; they are mostly considered residential areas organized to perform communal functions (Berger, 1978, pp. 53–54). It can be autonomous or part of a bigger system, with its own institutions, which can overlap with those of a larger geographical unit (Mancilla, 2017).

A *city* is "a relatively large, dense, and permanent settlement of heterogeneous individuals or groups of individuals organized to perform, or facilitate the performance of locality-relevant functions in an integrated manner and to ensure the integration of performance of these functions with the social system of which the city is part" (Berger, 53). The city tends to be interdependent with other similar units as part of a larger whole (Mancilla, 2017).

The term *region/federative entity* is used to distinguish the implementation of a central or federal model in a polity. In the case of a central system, a region is a territory that encompasses a series of cities and communities, whose administration is dependent on national policies. In the case of a federal system, a federative entity is a governmental subunit which comprises a territory that comprises a series of cities and communities, and possesses a much larger degree of autonomy from the central government than the region (Feeley, Rubin, 2008, p. 13).

A *state* is "a political community whose coherence and unity is established by the explicit identification, articulation and ordering of certain principles of norms ..." (Dyson, 1980, p. 212). A *confederacy of states* is the formal alliance of several states, and unlike the federal state, in a confederacy the degree of cohesion of the member units is minor – that is, they tend to possess broader autonomy, although they are still bound by the policies of the collective institutions. A contemporary example is the European Union, which is composed of 27 sovereign states, which possess a single market and a common currency, and other institutions that span from environmental policy and development to human rights (Europa).

The last configuration lies within what Wallerstein defines as a *world system*: "… a system *that is* a world and that can be, most often has been, located in an area less than the entire globe. World-systems analysis argues that the unities of social reality within which we operate, whose rules constrain us, are for the most part, such world-systems …" (Wallerstein, 2004, p. 98).

Geographical persons interact with the mobile in the following way: they constitute with their coercive rules over a territory, a field in which mobile persons must abide to operate and benefit from their resources or whatever the thing is that interests them; when they do so, they might seek to influence the rules of the field when it is not convenient. Both types of persons have a specific role in the world system, which empowers and constrains them, and they might be at an advantage or disadvantage depending on the way the rules have been configured or reconfigured (Mancilla, 2017).

A differentiation made between actors who hold stakes over a territory, and those that can move from one to another, or that can have a presence over many places at once, seems at first glance to have the notion of mobility in mind. I will understand this idea as the capacity of a social system to transport resources and people from one place to another (Mancilla, 2017).

Mobility has been important throughout human history. For example, in the Roman Empire troops moved from one region to the next, factory towns produced a single product and depended entirely on trade, while educated and trained people gravitated towards the capital. Developments in mobility center on the tension between the velocity in which resources (material and human) can be mobilized, and the cost of performing such an act; these two contribute greatly towards the increasing intercommunication of the world and the idea of the world system (Mancilla, 2017).

Communication and mobility are vital in the centralization of decisions. However, as interrelation of the world increases, so does the sheer volume and complexity of overall communications, which will always impede fully centralized and controlled decision-making. However, this is not the paradigm that sustains the geographic/mobile distinction; rather, it is *presence* (Mancilla, 2017).

The way in which territorial agents constitute themselves is based on their continued influence over a spatial extension and their ability to do so; mobile agents like organizations and organizational fields can reconstitute themselves in a territory different from the one in which they operate. Multinational corporations like GE can hold operations in over 100 countries, meaning that they are constrained by several territorial norms, but not completely by any one of them (Mancilla, 2017).

Presence, the ability to influence or operate in one or more territories, as well as mobilize from one to another *is the paradigm of the geographical/ mobile distinction*. Mobility is a central feature of presence as it results from the productive endeavors of each actor and also of their day-to-day operations (Mancilla, 2017).

Part 7: Recasting Constitutionalism

1 *Constitutionalism*

1.1 A Generic Model

We can understand constitutionalism generically as a model for political organization in which government is to be limited in its powers, with its authority dependent on the observation of these boundaries. The idea itself has a socio-historical context, for it stems from Locke and the Founding Generation of the United States (Stanford Encyclopedia of Philosophy, Constitutionalism).

In my article "Rethinking Constitutionalism: Using Epistemology to Show the Inadequacy of the Public/Private Distinction" I cited Horwitz on the fact that during the 1920s and '30s, legal philosophers belonging to the Legal Realist Movement attacked the foundations of the public/private distinction; scholars like Holmes, Brandeis, Hohfeld, Llewellyn, Pound and Cardozo devoted themselves to the effort, and others continue to seventy years later over it merely existing. But what makes it so? (Mancilla, 2017).

The reason for this is that constitutionalism has a set of presuppositions that function in a mutual, circular causal relation, which is recursive in nature: Constitutionalism needs and presupposes the existence of these elements and the latter depends on the former as well. These component parts are (Preuss, 2012, p. 23; Stanford Encyclopedia of Philosophy, Constitutionalism):

1. *Statehood*: Constitutions bring forth the creation of a state, which at the same time holds power over a territory. All states have constitutions and all states are constitutional states.
2. *Sovereignty*: The exclusive control over a territory.
3. *Separation of powers*: The exercise of state power is performed by organs charged with making new laws (legislative), implementing laws (executive) and adjudicating disputes under laws (judiciary).
4. *Public/private distinction*: In order to limit sovereign power, first it must be distinguished from what pertains to the individual.
5. *International/national distinction*: There are many states with their own constitutions and legal systems. The relationship between states is ruled by treaties, customs and in general, by international law.

We have, then, that a generic model of constitutionalism entails the control of power in a national state enacted through a constitution, which holds relationships with others alike, and is bound by international law without losing sovereignty. Such a state has a clear tripartite division of powers that can either be the distribution of clear-cut functions or the conferring of power to specialized organs ("branches" in this case); at the same time, there is a clear-cut division of what pertains to the polity and what to citizens, with the former being the strong party in a relationship between both.

1.2 Critique

The first thing to understand is that constitutionalism purports to be an effective limit to power. However, this idea ignores the realities of current times: powerful corporations that have a larger GDP than states and that can have a presence in virtually any of them; states that cede a part of their sovereignty in order to form part of a larger organ, or to be under a jurisdiction of an international court; and there are also public consequences of the actions of private actors, which can even violate constitutional rights.

As was said, current constitutionalism has as a sociohistorical context the realities of a time where the state was the most powerful social entity; thus, to limit power was to limit the state. Statehood as a paradigm of constitutionalism is in crisis due to phenomena that blur what were before defined boundaries.

Sovereignty is understood as the use of authority and force to enforce the territorial limits and interests of a state; however, there have been complex phenomena where states, corporations and even terrorist organizations and organized crime have asserted themselves in a territory. This means that the spatial limits of the states are not ineffable, nor the power of the polity insurmountable. Separation of powers is a form of political organization that is outdated, as the exercise of governmental power as the latter transcends three types of organs or three types of functions.

The public/private distinction has been increasingly blurred during the past decades, as we have seen the rise of corporate power, and the delegation of functions by states to corporations in order to cut expenses, as in the case of private prisons in the United States. There have been cases of corporations found in breach of constitutional rights, and there exist things such as political parties, which are private organizations but have public transcendence as they are vehicles to access power.

The international/national distinction weakened over the course of the 20th century as international organs that can act above the self-determination of states were created. Organs like the United Nations, the Organization of

American States and the European Union exist for a problem-solving reason: states gave up a measure of sovereign rights in order to have organisms that solved problems that could not be handled by a single state on the national level (Grimm, 2012, p. 16; Centre for Research on Globalization).

2 *An Alternative Model: Complex Constitutionalism*

Technological advances have unified the world in a way that was not considered possible decades ago, and that was essentially science fiction at the turn of the 19th century. Thus, we are in need of a new context for a political theory for and from the 21st century. *Constitutionalism as an effective limitation on power must account for international organizations and corporations.*

This, however, does not render the constitution obsolete: If one is to view constitutionalism solely from the perspective of statehood and sovereignty, one would contemplate a state of decline; when viewed holistically, *constitutionalism is merely part of a more complex sociopolitical order.*

Sovereignty must change from being in the territory to the attribute that people have to organize themselves into a distinct social entity; it is the capacity they have to assign a value to things and people and give them a role. What a constitution is should change from being the formal document by means of which a state creates or recreates itself, to the way in which any social entity or actor creates and maintains itself and the way it exercises power.

Constitutionalism as the creation, structuring and limitation of power, and its exercise and authority *changes radically under a mobile/geographic distinction*: There can be a general constitutionalism and particular constitutionalism(s). The first applies to aspects of creation and the limitation of power that concerns all social arrangements; the second pertains to aspects of particular social configurations.

Complex adaptive systems have the following features: 1) a complex system has many parts (or items, units, or individuals); 2) there are many relationships/interactions between the parts; and 3) the parts produce combined effects (synergies) that are not easily foreseen and may often be novel or surprising (chaotic) (Northrop, 2010, p. 2). There are then new constitutionalisms that can encompass groups as varied as tribes, organized religions, corporations, cities, states, and even organized crime, among others, and can be understood using the *3 by 3 by 3 model*, as well as the Viable System Model, which applies to all types of organizations.

The limitation (or lack) of power and authority in the world system constitutes a complex system, which I will call *complex constitutionalism*, and it consists of the interaction of particular constitutionalism(s) – which can sometimes complement and sometimes encroach upon each other – within the context of general constitutionalism.

The interaction of particular and general constitutionalism can be seen from three levels of analysis: a *macro* one, where the world system is comprised of many interacting constitutionalisms; a *meso* one that comprises the interrelation of two or more constitutionalisms; and a *micro* one that comprises the relation between a constitutionalism with respect to general constitutionalism and the world system. Complex constitutionalism goes beyond the sum of its parts, which cannot be understood as isolated wholes, and can be modeled in several ways, one of them being a network (Northrop, 2010, p. 5).

This concludes the endeavor of bringing forth a notion of constitutionalism suitable for the intricacies and sociohistorical context of current times. It is necessary to reconcile political theory with cybernetics and this is just a small step in such a direction – much debate and research is still needed.

Conclusions to Section 2

Cybernetics can lead to a more current constitutionalism; to call it "better" is a mistake, as the one that we have is a product of its time and has solved a wide array of problems posited by human sociability, to function to this day. There is no perfect framework, but there is always room for improvement. As it is said: Perfection is the enemy of the good.

One of the main flaws of current constitutionalism is the fact that it conceives of the limitation of power regarding the state, instead of seeing that there are non-territorial entities that have larger GDPs than some countries, and that there are international NGOs and authorities. That is, it seems to overlook international law and global governance.

Complex constitutionalism seeks to extend the idea of the limitation of power within all social structures, and in that respect, it benefits from the latter part of the *3 by 3 by 3 model*, which delves into human sociability, cutting through levels of analysis.

And as it was said before, this version of constitutionalism takes into its core living beings: We have a state that has a capacity to act vis-à-vis an environment that presents a series of problems; a constitutional order that is made and remade as it is applied; a division of functions within the different organs that comprise the state and which are visualized as a network; and a distinction between geographical and mobile actors that can span across the world system.

The political theory that Rubin denounced as inadequate (as do I) was too rigid and based on the state, which before held utmost importance, but now is a node in an extensive network of actors. What is offered in this section seeks to understand dynamic actors in a vast world, and could even be the basis of computer models.

General Conclusions

The purpose of the recasting effort is not only to bring forth a brand of political theory suitable for a globalized world that faces pandemics, climate change and world politics at an unprecedented scale, but also to help the reader see the assumptions that we make in our understanding of how we relate to one another socially.

This study presents a functional core of constitutionalism, but it is a work in progress, as the one we have now was assimilated and replicated over the course of numerous years and theorized by many. An example of this is the public/private distinction: All states have that notion in their constitutional framework, but each understands it in a different way, for in Mexico prisons cannot be private, yet they are in the United States.

To work, complex constitutionalism needs to be assimilated into all the social systems that we deemed it applicable to, and would also have to be extended to many other aspects that were left untreated because of space constraints.

For instance, at the Law and Society Association Conference of 2016, the topic of my presentation was the limitations of the state of emergency, based on the fact that human cognition is designed towards imminent threats and not towards slowly manifesting ones, that progress over a long period of time. This can be a topic for the expansion of complex constitutionalism; not only is there room for improvement, but also for development.

International theory can also benefit from the incorporation of cybernetics into its theories, and complex systems and networks can be used to understand something as dynamic and expansive as a world system. We live in an age of great technological advancements, most of which started with the ideas developed in the Macy Conferences; since then, social theory has been lagging behind, and we might as well use cybernetics to catch up.

Author's Note

This paper reunites a series of reflections that I have made over the years, both in what pertains to sociocybernetics and constitutional theory. I used some insights from my three-part article "Introduction to Sociocybernetics", published in the *Journal of Sociocybernetics*; I also drew from "Theorization and Modelling of Law: Some meso to macro models of legal behavior" published in *Ancilla Iuris*. I should also note that a part of the introductory section and that pertaining the public/private distinction was first published as an article called "Rethinking Constitutionalism: Using Epistemology to Show the Inadequacy of the Public/Private Distinction" in volume 17, issue 1 of *Global Jurist*.

On my brand of sociocybernetics, I must say that my foundation is first- and second-order cybernetics, mainly von Foerster, Maturana and Varela, Beer and Ashby, mixed with the biosemiotics of the Copenhagen-Tartu School, Robert Northrop's approach to complexity and Forrester and Meadows' systems theory.

Illustrations were made by Marco Antonio Flores and they followed the aesthetics that can be seen in the many handmade designs that Stafford Beer has in his books.

References

Bibliographical

Arnsten, A.F. (2009) 'Stress signaling pathways that impair prefrontal cortex structure and function', *Nature Reviews Neuroscience*, June, volume 10, issue 6.

Ashby, W.R. (1965) *Introduction to Cybernetics*, London: Chapman Hall Ltd.

Beer, S. (2012) *Brain of the Firm*, (2nd ed.), Hoboken: John Wiley and Sons.

Berger, P.L., Luckmann, T. (1967) *The Social Construction of Reality*, Anchor.

Bergson, H., (1920) *Creative Evolution*, London: Macmillan and Co. Limited.

von Bertalanffy, L. (1969) *General System Theory*, New York: George Braziller.

Bobbio, N., (1989) *Estado, Derecho y Sociedad*, Ciudad de México: FCE.

Bourgine, P., Lesne, A. (2006) *Morphogenesis: Origins of Patterns and Shapes*, New York: Springer.

Brest, P., (1986), 'Constitutional Interpretation' in *Encyclopedia of the American Constitution*, (Levy, L.W., Karst, K.L., Mahoney D.J. (eds.), New York: Macmillan Publishing Company.

Borja, R. (1991) *Derecho político y constitucional* (2nd. ed.), Ciudad de México: Fondo de Cultura Económica.

Brier, S. (2008) *Cybersemiotics: Why Information Is Not Enough*, Toronto: University of Toronto Press.

Burdeau, G., (1992) *L'Etat*, Machencourt: Editions du Seuil.

Carmona Tinoco, J.U., (1996) *La interpretación judicial constitucional* Ciudad de México: UNAM, Comisión Nacional de Derechos Humanos.

Castells, M., (2009) *Communication Power*, New York: Oxford.

del Castillo del Valle, A., (2004) *Defensa jurídica de la Constitución en México (derecho procesal constitucional mexicano)* (3rd. ed.). Ciudad de México: Edición Cumorah A.C..

Chamberlain, S.R., Robbins, T.W. (2013) 'Noradrenergic modulation of cognition: therapeutic implications', *Journal of Psychopharmacology*, August, volume 27, issue 8.

Chandler, D. (2007) *Semiotics: The Basics*, (2nd ed.), Abingdon: Routhledge.

Cyert, R.M., March, J.G., (2012) *A Behavioral Theory of the Firm*, (2nd ed.), Hoboken: Blackwell.

Dau-Lin, H. (1998) *Mutación de la Constitución*, Verdu, P.L., Forster, C. (trans.), Onati: Instituto Vasco de la Administración Pública.

Deutsch, K., (1966) *The Nerves of Government*, The Free Press.

Digeser, P., (1992) 'The Fourth Face of Power', *The Journal of Politics*, Vol. 54, No. 4.

Dyson, K., (1980) *The State Tradition in Western Europe*, Martin Robertson.

Eco, U. *Semiotics and the Philosophy of Language*, Bloomington: Indiana University Press.

Elkins, Z., Ginsburg, T., Melton, J., (2009) *The Endurance of National Constitutions*, New York: Cambridge University Press.

Feeley, M.M., Rubin, E.L., (2008), *Federalism: Political Identity and Tragic Compromise*. Ann Arbor: University of Michigan Press.

Feibleman, J.K. (1970) *An Introduction to the Philosophy of Charles S. Peirce*, New York: MIT Press.

Fix Zamudio, H., Valencia Carmona, S., (2005) *Derecho constitucional mexicano y comparado*, Ciudad de México: Porrúa.

von Foerster, H. (1994) *The Beginning of Heaven and Earth Has No Name*, New York: Fordham University Press.

von Foerster, H. (2003) *Understanding Understanding*, New York: Springer.

Gallese, V., Keysers, C., Rizzolatti, G., (2004) 'A unifying view of the basis of social cognition' *Trends in Cognitive Science*, September, volume 8, issue 9.

García Pelayo, M., (1951) *Derecho constitucional comparado*, (2nd ed.), Madrid: Manuales de la Revista de Occidente.

Geyer, F., van der Zouwen, J. (eds.), (2001) *Sociocybernetics: Complexity, Autopoiesis and Observation of Social Systems*, Westport: Greenwood Press.

Gerovicth, S. (2002) *From Newspeak to Cyberspeak. A History of Soviet Cybernetics*, Cambridge: MIT Press.

Grimm, D. (2012), 'The Achievement of Constitutionalism and its Prospects in a Changed World' in *The Twilight of Constitutionalism?* ed. Dobner, P., Loughlin, M., New York: Oxford University Press.

Gros, C. (2008) *Complex and Adaptive Dynamical Systems*, New York: Springer.

Harvard Law Review (2008) 'Counterinsurgency and Constitutional Design', *Harvard Law Review*, volume 121, issue 2.

Hauriou, M., (1929) *Précis de droit constitutionnel*, (10th ed.), Paris: Librairie Recueil Sirey.

Hudson, C.G., (2010) *Complex systems and human behavior*, Chicago: Lyceum Books.

Joseph, R. 'Quantum Physics and the Multiplicity of Mind: Split-Brains, Fragmented Minds, Dissociation, Quantum Consciousness' in Penrose, R., Hameroff, S., Kak, S., (eds.), *Consciousness and the Universe: Quantum Physics, Evolution, Brain & Mind*, Cosmology Science Publishers.

Kadushin, C., (2012) *Understanding Social Networks: Theories, Concepts, and Findings*, New York: Oxford.

Kahneman, D., (2011) *Thinking, Fast and Slow*, New York: Farrar, Straus and Giroux.

Kelsen, H., (1990) *General Theory of Norms*, New York.

Kennedy, D., (1997) *A critique of adjudication (fin de siècle)*, Cambridge: Harvard University Press.

Koob, G.F., (1992) 'Drugs of abuse: anatomy, pharmacology and function of reward pathways', *Trends in Pharmacological Sciences*, May, volume 13, issue 5.

Kuhn, A. (1963) *The Study of Society: A Unified Approach*, R.D. Irwin.

Kuhn, T.S., (1996) *The Structure of Scientific Revolutions*, Chicago: University of Chicago Press.

Lasswell, H.D., Kaplan, A., (1951) *Power and Society: A Framework for Political Inquiry*, New Haven: Yale University Press.

Levy, L.W. (1986) 'Constitution' in *Encyclopedia of the American Constitution*, (Levy, L.W., Karst, K.L., Mahoney D.J. (eds.), New York: Macmillan Publishing Company.

Liska, J.J. (1996) *A General Introduction to the Semiotic of Charles Sanders Peirce*, Bloomington: Indiana University Press.

Livas, J. (1988) *Cibernetica, Estado y Derecho*, Ciudad de México: Ediciones Guernika.

Loewenstein, K., (1965) *Political Power and the Governmental Process*, (2nd ed.) Chicago: University of Chicago Press.

Magill, M.E., (2000), 'The Real Separation in Separation of Powers Law', *Virginia Law Review*, Volume 86, number 6.

Magill, M.E., (2001) 'Beyond Powers and Branches in Separation of Powers Law', *University of Pennsylvania Law Review*, volume 150, number 2.

Mancilla Castro, R.G., (2012) *Derecho adjetivo constitucional*, Ciudad de México: NOVUM.

Maturana, H.R., Varela, F.J. (2012) *Autopoiesis and Cognition: The Realization of the Living*, Dordrecht: D. Reidel Publishing Company.

Medina, E. (2011) *Cybernetic Revolutionaries*, Cambridge: MIT Press.

Modugno, F., (2004) *Teoría de la Interpretación Jurídica*, Querétaro: FUNDAP.

Montuori, A., (2008) '*Introduction*' in Morin, E. (2008) *On complexity*, Cresskill: Hampton Press.

Morilak, D.A., Barrera, G., Echevarria, D.J., Garcia, A.S., Hernandez, A. (2005) 'Role of brain norepinephrine in the behavioral response to stress', *Progress in Neuro-Psychopharmacology & Biological Psychiatry*, December, volume 29, issue 8.

Morin, E. (2008) *On complexity*, Cresskill: Hampton Press.

Morsella, E., Jantz, T., (2011). 'Conscious States Are a Crosstalk Mechanism for Only a Subset of Brain Processes' in Penrose, R., Hameroff, S., Kak, S., (eds.), *Consciousness and the Universe: Quantum Physics, Evolution, Brain & Mind*, Cosmology Science Publishers.

Mortati, C., (1969), *Istituzioni di diritto pubblico*, volume I, Padua: Cedam.

Naranjo Mesa, V., (2006) *Teoría constitucional e instituciones políticas,* (10th. ed.), Bogotá: Temis.

Nogueira Alcalá, H., (2007) 'La dignidad humana, los derechos fundamentales, el bloque constitucional de derechos fundamentales y sus garantìas jurisdiccionales', *Gaceta Jurídica – Chile*, No. 322.

Nonet, P., Selznick, P. (1978) *Law and Society in Transition: Toward Responsive Law*, New York: Harper & Row Publishers.

Northrop, R.B. (2010) *Introduction to Complexity and Complex systems*, Boca Raton: CRC Press.

Ohio State University, *Language Files: Materials for an Introduction to Language and Linguistics*, Mihalicek, V., Wilson, C. (eds.), (11th ed.), Columbus: Ohio State University Press.

Osiatyński, W., (2009) *Human Rights and Their Limits,* Cambridge: Cambridge University Press.

Piaget, J., (1974) *Seis Estudios de Psicologia*, Nuria Petit (trans.), Barcelona: Editorial Seix Barral.

Pickering, A. (2010), *The Cybernetic Brain. Sketches of Another Future*, University of Chicago Press.

Powell, W.W., DiMaggio, P.J., (1991) 'The Iron Cage Revisited: Institutional Isomorphism and Collective Rationality in Organizational Fields', in *The New Institutionalism in Organizational Analysis*, Powell, W.W., DiMaggio, P.J. (eds.), Chicago: University of Chicago Press.

Preuss, U.K., (2012) 'Disconnecting Constitutions from Statehood, Is Global Constitutionalism a Viable Concept?' in *The Twilight of Constitutionalism?* ed. Dobner, P., Loughlin, M., New York: Oxford University Press.

Radin, D., (1997) *The Conscious Universe*, San Francisco: Harper One.

Reyes, A., Espejo, R., (2011), *Organizational Systems: Managing Complexity with the Viable System Model*, New York: Springer.

Richerson, P.J., Boyd, R. (2005) *Not by genes alone: How culture transformed human evolution*, Chicago: University of Chicago Press.

Robles, G., (1982) *Las reglas del Derecho y las reglas de los Juegos. Ensayo de Teoría analítica del Derecho*, Madrid.

Rubin, E. (2005) *Beyond Camelot*, Princeton: Princeton University Press.

Schmitt, C., (2006) *Teoría de la Constitución*, (5th reprint,), Ayala, F., (trans.), Madrid: Alianza Editorial.

Serra Rojas, A., (1964) *Teoría general del Estado*, Ciudad de México: Porrúa.

Scott, W.R. and Davis, G.F., (2007) *Organizations and Organizing*. Pearson, Prentice Hall.

Searle, J.R., (2010) *Making the Social World*, New York: Oxford University Press.

Selznick, P., Broom, L., Broom Darroch, D., (1981) *Sociology*, (7th ed.), New York: Harper and Row.

Shevrin, H. 'What does Consciousness do?' in Penrose, R., Hameroff, S., Kak, S., (eds.), *Consciousness and the Universe: Quantum Physics, Evolution, Brain & Mind*, Cosmology Science Publishers.

Stillings, N.A., Weisler, S.E., Chase, C., Feinstein, M.H., Garfield, J.L., Rissland, E.L., (1995) *Cognitive Science. An Introduction*, (2nd ed.) New York: MIT Press.

Tamanaha, B.Z. (2004) *On the rule of law: History, politics, theory*, New York: Cambridge University Press.

Trueba Urbina, A. (1951) *¿Qué es una constitución político-social?*, Ciudad de México: Editorial Ruta.

Twining, W., (2009) *General Jurisprudence: Understanding Law from a Global Perspective*, Cambridge: Cambridge University Press.

Uddin, L.Q., Iacoboni, M., Lange, C., Keenan, J.P., (2007) 'The self and social cognition: the role of cortical midline structures and mirror neurons', *Trends in Cognitive Sciences*, April, volume 11, issue 4.

Van Hoecke, M., (2002) *Law as Communication*, London: Hart Publishing, 2002.

Varela, F.J., Thompson, E., Rosch, E. (1993) *The Embodied Mind: Cognitive Science and Human Experience*, New York: MIT Press.

Verdú, P.L., (1998) *Teoría de la constitución como ciencia cultural*, (2nd ed.), Madrid: Dykinson.

Wallerstein, I. (2004) *World-Systems Analysis: An Introduction*. Durham: Duke University Press.

Walton, D., (2004) *Abductive Reasoning*, Tuscaloosa: University of Alabama Press.

Wiener, N. (1961) *Cybernetics: Or Control and Communication in the Animal and the Machine*, (2nd ed.) New York: MIT Press.

Zaluski, W., (2013) *Game Theory in Jurisprudence*, Copernicus Center Press.

Electronic

Bandes, S.A., Blumenthal, J.A., (2012) 'Emotion and the Law', *Annual Review of Law and Social Science*, volume 8, Available at: https://doi.org/10.1146/annurev-lawsocsci-102811-173825 (Accessed: 20 January 2020).

Berger, A.S., (1978) *The City: Urban Communities and Their Problems*. [Online]. Available at: http://books.google.com/books?id=INcgTPo-U1cC&printsec=frontcover#v=onepage&q&f=false

Block, N., *On a confusion about a function of consciousness* [Online]. Available at: http://cogprints.org/231/1/199712004.html (Accessed: 20 January 2020).

Business Insider (2011) '25 US Mega Corporations: Where They Rank If They Were Countries'. [Online]. Available at: http://www.businessinsider.com/25-corporations-bigger-tan-countries-2011-6?op=1#ixzz3VFPE3VoC (Accessed: 20 January 2020).

Calhoun, R., Hayward, B.F., (2007) 'Stabilising Complex Adaptive Systems Using Complexity Theory In Operational Design For Stabilisation And Support Operations', *Australian Army Journal*, volume VII, number 3. Available at: https://researchcentre.army.gov.au/sites/default/files/aaj_2010_3.pdf (Accessed: 20 January 2020).

Centre for Research on Globalization, (2008) 'The Prison Industry in the United States: Big Business or a New Form of Slavery?'. [Online]. Available at: http://www.globalresearch.ca/the-prison-industry-in-the-united-states-big-business-or-a-new-form-of-slavery/8289 (Accessed: 20 January 2020).

Claus, L., (2004) 'Montesquieu's Mistakes and the True Meaning of Separation'. *University of San Diego Legal Working Paper Series. University of San Diego Public Law and Legal Theory Research Paper Series*. Working Paper 11. Available at: http://law.bepress.com/sandiegolwps/pllt/art11 (Accessed: 20 January 2020).

Conant, C., Ashby, W.R., (1970) 'Every Good Regulator of a System Must be a Model of That System', *International Journal of Systems Science*, volume 1, Number 2. Available at: http://pespmc1.vub.ac.be/books/Conant_Ashby.pdf (Accessed: 20 January 2020).

Colby, C.L., (2001) 'Perception of Extrapersonal Space: Psychological and Neural Aspects', *ScienceDirect*, Available at: https://www.sciencedirect.com/topics/computer-science/spatial-perception (Accessed: 20 January 2020).

Engle, E. (2009) 'Third Party Effect of Fundamental Rights (Drittwirkung)', *Hanse Law Review*, volume 5, Number 2, (2009) Available at: https://papers.ssrn.com/sol3/papers.cfm?abstract_id=1481552 (Accessed: 20 January 2020)

EUROPA, *About the EU* EUROPA. [Online]. Available at: https://europa.eu/european-union/about-eu_en (Accessed: 20 January 2020).

von Foerster, H., *Cybernetics of Cybernetics, 1979* [Online]. Available at: http://jlombardi.net/pdf/cyber_cyber.pdf (Accessed: 20 January 2020).

Gözler, K. (2008) *Judicial Review of Constitutional Amendments: A Comparative Study*, Bursa: Ekin Press, Available at: http://www.anayasa.gen.tr/jrca.pdf (Accessed: 20 January 2020).

García Roca, J., (2000) 'Del Principio de la división de poderes', *Revista de Estudios Politicos*, April-June, number 108. Available at: https://dialnet.unirioja.es/descarga/articulo/27611.pdf (Accessed: 20 January 2020).

Ginsburg, T. Comparative Constitutional Review, *United States Institute of Peace*. [Online]. Available at: https://www.usip.org/sites/default/files/ROL/TG_Memo_on_Constitutional_Review%20for%202011_v4.pdf (Accessed: 20 January 2020).

Harris, L.R., Carnevale, M.J., D'Amour, S., Fraser, L.E., Harrar, V., Hoover, A.E.N., Mander, C., Pritchett, L.M. 'How our body influences our perception of the world',

Frontiers in Psychology, Available at: https://www.frontiersin.org/articles/10.3389/fpsyg.2015.00819/full (Accessed: 20 January 2020).

Heylighen, F., Joslyn, C., (2001) 'Cybernetics and Second-Order Cybernetics', in Meyers, R.A. (ed.), *Encyclopedia of Physical Science & Technology* (3rd ed.), New York: Academic Press. Available at: http://pespmc1.vub.ac.be/Papers/Cybernetics-EPST.pdf (Accessed: 20 January 2020).

Horwitz, M.J. (1982) 'The History of the Public/Private Distinction', *University of Pennsylvania Law Review*, volume 130, issue 6. Available at: http://scholarship.law.upenn.edu/cgi/viewcontent.cgi?article=4677&context=penn_law_review (Accessed: 20 January 2020).

International Committee of the Red Cross. 'Privatization of War' [Online]. Available at: https://www.icrc.org/en/document/privatization-war (Accessed: 20 January 2020).

International Covenant on Civil and Political Rights, (1966) [Online]. Available at: http://www.hrcr.org/docs/Civil&Political/intlcivpol5.html (Accessed: 20 January 2020).

International Covenant on Economic, Social and Cultural Rights, (1966) [Online]. Available at: http://www.ohchr.org/EN/ProfessionalInterest/Pages/CESCR.aspx (Accessed: 20 January 2020).

Kennedy, D. (1982) 'The Stages of the Decline of the Public/Private Distinction', *University of Pennsylvania Law Review*, volume 130, issue 6. Available at: http://scholarship.law.upenn.edu/cgi/viewcontent.cgi?article=4675&context=penn_law_review (Accessed: 20 January 2020).

Klare, K.E., (1982) 'The Public/Private Distinction in Labor Law', *University of Pennsylvania Law Review*, volume 130, issue 6. Available at: http://scholarship.law.upenn.edu/cgi/viewcontent.cgi?article=4676&context=penn_law_review (Accessed: 20 January 2020).

Kuhn, R. (2015), 'Internal Migration: Developing Countries', *ScienceDirect*, Available at: https://www.sciencedirect.com/topics/social-sciences/internal-migration (Accessed: 20 January 2020).

Mancilla, R. (2011) 'Introduction to Sociocybernetics (Part 1): Third order cybernetics and a basic framework for society', *Journal of Sociocybernetics*, volume 9, number 1/2. Available at: https://papiro.unizar.es/ojs/index.php/rc51-jos/article/download/623/633 (Accessed: 20 January 2020).

Mancilla, R. (2012) 'Introduction to Sociocybernetics part 2: Power, Culture and Institutions', *Journal of Sociocybernetics*, volume 10. Available at: https://papiro.unizar.es/ojs/index.php/rc51-jos/article/view/625 (Accessed: 20 January 2020).

Mancilla, R. (2015) 'Theorization and Modelling of Law', *Ancilla Iuris*. Available at: https://www.anci.ch/articles/ancilla2015_155_mancilla.pdf (Accessed: 20 January 2020).

Mancilla, R. (2017), 'Rethinking Constitutionalism: Using Epistemology to Show the Inadequacy of the Public/Private Distinction' *Global Jurist*, April, volume 17, issue 1, Available at: https://www.degruyter.com/view/j/gj.2017.17.issue-1/gj-2015-0015/gj-2015-0015.xml?format=INT (Accessed: 20 January 2020).

Marchant, M.A., Snell, W.M. (1997), 'Macroeconomic and International Policy Terms', *University of Kentucky, College of Agriculture, Cooperative Extension Service*, Available at: http://www2.ca.uky.edu/agcomm/pubs/aec/aec75/aec75.pdf (Accessed: 20 January 2020).

Morin, E., *Restricted complexity, general complexity*, [Online]. Available at: http://cogprints.org/5217/1/Morin.pdf (Accessed: 20 January 2020).

Monroy Cabra, M.G., (2005) 'Concepto de Constitución', *Anuario de Derecho Constitucional Latinoamericano*, volume 1., number 20051. Available at: http://historico.juridicas.unam.mx/publica/librev/rev/dconstla/cont/20051/pr/pr3.pdf (Accessed: 20 January 2020).

Montuori, A., *Complex Thought. An Overview of Edgar Morin's Intellectual Journey*. [Online]. Available at: http://www.academia.edu/4074758/COMPLEX_THOUGHT_An_Overview_of_Edgar_Morins_Intellectual_Journey (Accessed: 20 January 2020).

Oxford Dictionary, *Order*, [Online]. Available at: https://www.lexico.com/definition/order (Accessed: 20 January 2020).

Oxford Dictionary, *Pattern*, [Online]. Available at: https://www.lexico.com/definition/pattern (Accessed: 20 January 2020).

Oxford Dictionary, *Balance*, [Online]. Available at: https://www.lexico.com/definition/balance (Accessed: 20 January 2020).

Oxford Dictionary, *Proportion*, [Online]. Available at: https://www.lexico.com/definition/proportion (Accessed: 20 January 2020).

Oxford University, (2017) 'The amazing phenomenon of muscle memory', Medium, Available at: https://medium.com/oxford-university/the-amazing-phenomenon-of-muscle-memory-fb1cc4c4726 (Accessed: 20 January 2020).

Peters, B. (2012) 'Normalizing Soviet Cybernetics', *Information & Culture: A Journal of History*, Volume 47, Number 2, *2012*, [Online]. Available at: http://nevzlin.huji.ac.il/userfiles/files/47.2.peters.pdf (Accessed: 20 April 2020).

Principia Cybernetica Web, *Cybernetics*, [Online]. Available at: http://pespmc1.vub.ac.be/ASC/CYBERNETICS.html (Accessed: 20 April 2020).

Principia Cybernetica Web, *Feedback*, [Online]. Available at: http://pespmc1.vub.ac.be/FEEDBACK.html (Accessed: 20 January 2020).

Principia Cybernetica Web, *Homeostasis*, [Online]. Available at: http://pespmc1.vub.ac.be/HOMEOSTA.html

Principia Cybernetica Web, *The Law of Requisite Variety*, [Online]. Available at: http://pespmc1.vub.ac.be/REQVAR.html (Accessed: 20 January 2020).

Principia Cybernetica Web, *Order from noise*, [Online]. Available at: http://pespmc1.vub.ac.be/ORDNOISE.html

Principia Cybernetica Web, *Self-organization*, [Online]. Available at: http://pespmc1.vub.ac.be/SELFORG.html

Principia Cybernetica Web, *What is Complexity?* [Online]. Available at: http://pespmc1.vub.ac.be/COMPLEXI.html (Accessed: 20 January 2020).

Sagüés, N.P., (2007) 'Problemática de los órganos extrapoder en el diagrama de la división de poderes' *Anuario de Derecho Constitucional Latinoamericano*, volume II., number 20072. Available at: https://www.kas.de/c/document_library/get_file?uuid=16fe1960-8207-7a82-5a14-07a0b0ab9e79&groupId=271408 (Accessed: 20 January 2020).

Santa Fe Institute, *History*, [Online]. Available at: https://www.santafe.edu/about/history (Accessed: 20 January 2020).

Scholten, D.L., *Every Good Doctor Must Represent the Patient: The Malfunction of Evidence-Based Medicine* [Online]. Available at: http://orthomolecular.org/resources/omns/v08n01.shtml (Accessed: 20 January 2020).

Sohm, R. *The Institutes of Roman Law*. [Online]. Available at: https://archive.org/stream/cu31924017749064/cu31924017749064_djvu.txt (Accessed: 20 January 2020)

Stanford Encyclopedia of Philosophy, (2001) *Constitutionalism*, [Online]. Available at: https://plato.stanford.edu/entries/constitutionalism/ (Accessed: 20 January 2020).

Stanford Encyclopedia of Philosophy, (2000) *The Experience and Perception of Time*, [Online]. Available at: https://plato.stanford.edu/entries/time-experience/ (Accessed: 20 January 2020).

Stanford Encyclopedia of Philosophy, (2004) *Henri Bergson*, [Online]. Available at: http://plato.stanford.edu/entries/bergson/ (Accessed: 20 January 2020).

Stanford Encyclopedia of Philosophy, (2002) *The Pure Theory of Law*, [Online]. Available at: http://plato.stanford.edu/entries/lawphil-theory/#BasNor (Accessed: 20 January 2020).

Tomás y Valiente, F., (1994) *La Resistencia constitucional y los valores*, [Online]. Available at: http://www.cervantesvirtual.com/descargaPdf/la-resistencia-constitucional-y-los-valores/ (Accessed: 20 January 2020).

Umpleby, S.A., *What comes after second order cybernetics?*, 2001, [Online]. Available at: http://www.nomads.usp.br/pesquisas/design/objetos_interativos/arquivos/restrito/umpleby_what_comes_after_second_order_cybernetics.pdf (Accessed: 20 April 2020).

El Universal, (2019) *Congreso declara constitucional reforma que reconoce a los afromexicanos* [Online]. Available at: https://www.eluniversal.com.mx/nacion/politica/congreso-declara-constitucional-reforma-que-reconoce-los-afromexicanos (Accessed: 20 January 2020).

Universal Declaration of Human Rights, (1948) [Online]. Available at: https://www.un.org/en/universal-declaration-human-rights/index.html (Accessed: 20 January 2020).

University of Washington, *Neuroscience for kids*, [Online]. Available at: https://faculty.washington.edu/chudler/cells.html (Accessed: 20 January 2020).

Zeitlin, M.F., Megawangi, R., Kramer, E.M., Colletta, N.D., Babatunde, E.D., Garman, D., *Strengthening the family – Implications for international development*, [Online]. Available at: http://www.nzdl.org/gsdlmod?e=d-00000-00---off-0hdl--00-0----0-10-0---0---0direct-10---4-------0-1l--11-en-50---20-about---00-0-1-00-0--4----0-0-11-10-0utfZz-8-00&cl=CL1.16&d=HASHb09285b7bcd64b52bb9ac7.3.3&gt=1 (Accessed: 20 January 2020).

www.ingramcontent.com/pod-product-compliance
Lightning Source LLC
Chambersburg PA
CBHW031328230926
51848CB00001B/139
* 9 7 8 9 0 0 4 4 4 0 9 8 2 *